XSL:

The Personal Trainer for XSLT, XPath and XSL-FO

William R. Stanek

PUBLISHED BY

Stanek & Associates
PO Box 362
East Olympia, WA 98540-0362

United States of America

Cover Design: Creative Designs Ltd.
Editorial Development: Andover Publishing Solutions
Technical Review: L & L Technical Content Services

You can provide feedback related to this book by emailing the author at williamstanek@aol.com. Please use the name of the book as the subject line.

Contents at a Glance

Table of Contents

Introduction

XSL: The Personal Trainer for XSLT, XPath and XSL-FO is an authoritative quick reference guide to the Extensible Stylesheet Language (XSL) and is designed to be a key resource you turn to whenever you have questions about XSL. To this end, the book zeroes in on the key aspects of XSLT, XPath and XSL-FO that you'll use the most.

Inside this book's pages, you'll find comprehensive overviews, step-by-step procedures, frequently used tasks, documented examples, and much more. One of the goals is to keep the content so concise that the book remains compact and easy to navigate while at the same time ensuring that the book is packed with as much information as possible—making it a valuable resource.

What is this Book About?

XSL: The Personal Trainer for XSLT, XPath and XSL-FO focuses on the essentials and provides discussions of key related technologies that you'll need to be successful. The book is designed for anyone who wants to learn XSL, including those who create or support XML-based solutions.

> **Note** If you have any questions about XML, be sure to look for XML, DTDs, Schemas: The Personal Trainer. XSL: The Personal Trainer for XSLT, XPath and XSL-FO was written to compliment XML, DTDs, Schemas: The Personal Trainer.

To pack in as much information as possible, I had to assume that you have basic technology skills and a basic understanding of the Internet, the World Wide Web, and markup languages, such as Hypertext Markup Language (HTML). With this in mind, I don't devote entire chapters to understanding the World Wide Web, markup languages, or how structured documents can be used on the Web. You should already know this material or have resources to study. I do, however, provide a detailed introduction to XSLT, XPath,

XSL-FO and their related technologies that serves as the start of your foray into the world of XSL. I also examine the structure of related documents.

As I stated, I assume that you're familiar with the Internet and the Web. For example, I might talk about transfer protocols, such as Hypertext Transfer Protocol (HTTP), in various contexts and assume that you know that HTTP is used to transfer information over the Web. I might also discuss documents that use HTML and compare them to documents that use XML. Again, I'll assume that you know the basics of HTML and the Web. If you don't (or have forgotten what you previously learned), I'd recommend getting a book that covers the basics of the Internet and the basics of Web publishing.

How Is This Book Organized?

XSL: The Personal Trainer for XSLT, XPath and XSL-FO is designed to be studied as a resource guide and used as a quick reference to meet your everyday needs when you are implementing or maintaining XML-based solutions. Speed and ease of reference is an essential part of this hands-on guide. The book has an expanded table of contents and many other quick reference features have been added as well. These features include quick step-by-step instructions, lists, and fast facts. The book is broken down into six chapters that examine techniques you can use to transform XML structures dynamically.

An understanding of transformation is essential if you want to implement or support an end-to-end XML solution. Typically, you'll use transformations to structure information dynamically after extracting the information from a database. Chapter 1 introduces XSL Transformations and related technologies, including XSL Formatting Objects (used to provide formatting and style) and XML Path (XPath) (used to identity parts of documents). Chapter 2 provides a detailed discussion of XPath operators and expressions that you can use to locate specific parts of XML documents. Chapter 3 examines structures that you can use to conditionally process a part of a document based on the value of an expression.

The advanced discussion of XSLT and XPath continues with Chapters 4, 5, and 6. Chapter 4 explores techniques you can use to pass values into templates and hold values temporarily during processing. Chapter 5 delves into techniques you can use to manipulate the text content of elements and attributes. You'll learn how to extract substrings, convert strings to number, format strings, and much more. Chapter 6 completes the discussion of XSLT and XPath by explaining how to restructure input documents and manipulate document subsets. You'll learn how to merge sets of documents, how to manipulate document structures, and how to define sort keys.

What Conventions Are Used in This Book?

I've used a variety of elements to help keep the text clear and easy to follow. You'll find code terms and listings in monospace type, except when I tell you to actually type a command. In that case, the command appears in bold type. When I introduce and define a new term, I put it in italics.

This book also has notes, tips and other sidebar elements that provide additional details on points that need emphasis.

I truly hope you find that *XSL: The Personal Trainer for XSLT, XPath and XSL-FO* helps you use XSL successfully and effectively. Keep in mind that throughout this guide, where I have used click, right-click and double-click, you can also use touch equivalents, tap, press and hold, and double tap.

Thank you,

William R. Stanek

(williamstanek@aol.com)

Chapter 1. XSL Transformations & Formatting

Extensible Stylesheet Language (XSL) defines rules that specify how to extract information from an XML document and how to format this information so that it can be viewed. XSL is divided into three parts:

- **XSL Transformations (XSLT)** A language for transforming XML documents
- **XML Path (XPath)** An expression language used by XSLT to access and refer to parts of a document
- **XSL Formatting Objects (XSL-FO)** An XML vocabulary used by XSLT to describe the formatting of text on a page

The focus of this chapter is XSLT. XSLT will remain the focus of the discussion throughout this part of the book. Chapter 2, "XPath Operators & Expressions," continues the XSLT discussion by detailing how to use XPath with XSLT. Chapter 3, "Branching & Control Functions," delves into many of the advanced features of XSLT and XPath. Chapter 4, "Variables & Parameters in XSLT," explores techniques for creating links and cross-references using XSLT.

Introducing XSLT

XSLT is a language for transforming XML documents. You use XSLT to specify the rules by which one XML document is transformed into another type of document. Although the output of the transformation process could be an XML document, it's more commonly an HTML document that's designed to be viewed by users. The output could also be a Unicode text file, a Portable Document File (PDF), a file containing programming code written in Java, Active Server Pages (ASP) or another programming language, or just about any other file type.

The typical transformation process starts with an input document that's matched against a set of one or more XSLT documents, called XSLT stylesheets. You write XSLT stylesheets to define the rules for transforming a specific type of XML document. During the transformation process, an XSLT processor analyzes the contents of the input document to match specific criteria defined in the stylesheet. These criteria are organized as templates that define actions to take when a match is found. When an XSLT processor determines that an element matches a template definition, it writes the contents of the template to an output buffer. Upon finishing the analysis, the processor might restructure the output buffer to format the document as XML, HTML, and so on.

XSLT is created to be more powerful and versatile than other stylesheet languages, such as cascading style sheets (CSS). Although you can use CSS with XML, it really isn't optimized to work with data. You can use CSS to specify font types, set margins, and position content, but you can't use CSS to perform many of the tasks you'll want to perform on data. Tasks that XSLT excels at include

- **Sorting** Allows you to change the order of elements according to a set of criteria. For example, you could sort a list of accounts alphabetically.
- **Filtering** Allows you to remove elements that aren't applicable in a specific context. For example, you could filter out incomplete orders from an order summary to show only orders that have been completed.
- **Calculating** Allows you to perform arithmetic functions. For example, you could total the sales proceeds from multiple orders.
- **Merging** Allows you to combine multiple documents into a single document. For example, you could combine all the sales orders for the month into a single summary document called Monthly Sales.

When you need to perform any of these tasks on data or perform standard transformations going from XML to another format, XSLT should be your tool of choice. Don't worry, if you need to apply formatting to a document after it's been transformed, you can still do this—I'll show you how later in the chapter.

Because a solid understanding of the transformation process is essential to working with XSLT, lets take a more detailed look at this process, starting with the following sample input document:

```
<?xml version="1.0"?>
<document>
XSLT is a powerful transformation language.
</document>
```

Although you can view an XML document directly in a Web browser or another application, the document isn't formatted. To format the document for viewing, you'd want to transform the document into another format, such as HTML. Here's an XSLT stylesheet that specifies how to transform the sample document:

```
<xsl:stylesheet version="2.0"
  xmlns:xsl="http://www.w3.org/1999/XSL/Transform">

  <xsl:output method="html"/>

  <xsl:template match="/">
    <xsl:apply-templates select="document"/>
  </xsl:template>

  <xsl:template match="document">
    <html>
      <body>
        <p>
          <xsl:value-of select="."/>
        </p>
      </body>
    </html>
  </xsl:template>

</xsl:stylesheet>
```

Tip All markup inserted into an XSLT stylesheet must be well formed, regardless of whether the markup is XML, HTML, or some other markup language. Thus, although HTML would allow you to enter only the opening paragraph tag <p>, you must enter both the opening and closing paragraph tags.

Although I'll examine XSLT stylesheets in detail shortly, let's focus on the basics for now. The first template in this stylesheet tells an XSLT processor to find the root element and apply the second template to any `document` elements in the source document. The second template replaces the begin <document> and end </document> tags with the HTML markup provided and then inserts the value of the `document` element into the HTML paragraph tag.

The result is the following HTML document:

```
<html>
<body>
<p>
  XSLT is a powerful transformation language.
</p>
</body>
</html>
```

As with XML processors, you can find a number of capable XSLT processors. Once you've installed a processor, you can use the processer to parse and transform documents. After you've transformed a file into a specific format, you can view the file in an appropriate application, such as a Web browser, to ensure that the transformation worked.

When working with XSLT, keep in mind that the only template automatically applied to any document is the template for the root node. All other templates must be invoked when a particular document structure matches a template rule. You must explicitly define expressions to determine which additional templates are applied. You do this by defining a root template that in turn invokes other templates.

Templates are always recursively processed. In this example the root template specifies that there are templates for three elements (`element1`, `element2`, and `element3`):

```
<xsl:stylesheet version="2.0"
  xmlns:xsl="http://www.w3.org/1999/XSL/Transform">

  <xsl:template match="/">
    <xsl:apply-templates select="element1"/>
    <xsl:apply-templates select="element2"/>
    <xsl:apply-templates select="element3"/>
  </xsl:template>
...
```

```
</xsl:stylesheet>
```

The XSLT processor would start with the root template and then process the template for `element1`. If the rules for `element1` invoked other templates, these templates would each be processed in turn. When the processor was finished recursively processing templates associated with `element1`, the processor would start with the rules for `element2`, and so on.

Matching Document Structures to Template Rules

Recursion is a powerful aspect of XSLT. When XSLT processors analyze input documents, they see document structures as node trees, where nodes represent individual pieces of the XML document, such as elements, attributes, text, comments, and processing instructions, and the node tree itself is a hierarchical representation of the entire XML document.

At the top of the node tree is the root node, which represents a document's root element. Top-level elements in a document become branches of the tree with the low-level elements that they contain below them. Any contents or attributes of elements are broken out in the tree structure as well. This makes the node tree easy to traverse as long as the processor understands the basic parent-child-sibling concepts discussed in *XML, DTDs, Schemas: The Personal Trainer* and knows how to locate various types of nodes using these concepts.

The actual underlying technology that enables document structures to be represented as node trees and traversed is XPath. XPath defines a set of standard nodes and provides the functions for locating those nodes. Node types defined by XPath are

- **Root** Represents the root element in XML documents (each document has only one root node). The root node contains the entire document. Although it has no parent nodes, all top-level nodes are its children and all nodes are its descendants.
- **Element** Represents all elements in XML documents, including root nodes. This means that element nodes exist for the root element and all other elements in a document. Elements nodes can have parents and children. The parent nodes are either the root node or another higher-level element node. Children nodes can include other element nodes, text nodes, comment nodes, and processing instruction nodes that occur within the element.

- **Attribute** Represents attributes in XML documents. Although element nodes are the parent of attribute nodes, attribute nodes aren't children of element nodes. This is a subtle but important semantic distinction between attribute nodes and other nodes. The reason for this distinction is that attribute nodes aren't present unless they're specifically requested. Once an attribute is requested, a node is added to the node tree and the value of the attribute can be read. This remains true if default values for attributes are defined in a document type definition (DTD) or schema but aren't explicitly specified in elements. Attributes inherited by an element from higher-level elements are also available. This applies to the `xml:lang` and `xml:space` attributes, which are applied to an element and inherited by its child elements. Keep in mind that the XML processor must be able to access external DTDs or schemas to determine that default values are defined and available. If the processor can't do this, the default values won't be available.
- **Text** Represents the text contents of elements. If any text associated with an element contains entity or character references, these references are resolved before the text node is created. CDATA sections in documents are represented as text nodes as well where the parent element is the element in which the CDATA section is defined. If the element containing the CDATA section is the root element, the root element will have a text node. If any element already has a text node, the contents of the CDATA section are added to the existing contents of the text node. This ensures that the text node contains the entire textual contents of the related element. Because references and CDATA sections are resolved before the text node is created, there's no way to determine that the text originally contained references or CDATA sections.
- **Comment** Represents comments inserted into XML documents. All comments inserted into a document become comment nodes (except for comments in a DTD or schema). The text of the comment is everything inside the comment except for the opening <!-- and closing -->, respectively.
- **Processing instruction** Represents processing instructions in XML documents. Processing instruction nodes contain two values: the name of the instruction, which can be obtained with the name() function, and a string containing the rest of the processing instruction, but not including the opening <? or closing ?>, respectively.
- **Namespace** Represents namespaces declared in XSLT stylesheets. Namespace nodes are used by the XSLT processor and aren't meant to be used by stylesheet developers. Namespace nodes contain the value assigned to an element's xmlns attribute. The xmlns attribute isn't represented as an attribute node.

Each of these node types has a built-in template rule associated with it that allows the node to be processed as necessary. The following sections examine these built-in template rules.

The Template for Element and Root Nodes

The built-in template for element and root nodes is used to process the root node and all of its child nodes. The template is defined as:

```
<xsl:template match="*|/">
   <xsl:apply-templates/>
</xsl:template>
```

As shown, the template match value is defined as:

```
*|/
```

These characters represent an XPath expression and all have special meaning:

- * is a wildcard character, indicating that any value is allowed. In the match attribute, this says match any element name.
- | is a choice indicator, indicating to match either by using the asterisk (*) or the slash (/).
- / is the designator for the root node. XPath refers to the root node using this designator.

Thus, when you put these characters together, all element nodes and the root node are deemed matches for the XPath expression. The xsl:apply-templates statement tells the XSLT processor to apply the appropriate templates to nodes in the input document. This ensures that any node in the document can be processed, even if there are no template rules for parent nodes.

The Template for Modes

The xsl:template element has a mode attribute that lets you process the same set of nodes using different template rules. The built-in template that ensures modes are recognized is:

```
<xsl:template match="*|/" mode="x">
   <xsl:apply-templates mode="x"/>
</xsl:template>
```

This template ensures that element and root nodes are processed regardless of the mode that's currently being used. The mode template is only invoked when you define modes in your XSLT stylesheet, and then the template only works to ensure that the various modes are recognized. You'll learn more about modes in Chapter 3.

The Template for Text and Attribute Nodes

The built-in template for text and attribute nodes ensures that these nodes can be processed regardless of their value. This template is defined as:

```
<xsl:template match="text()|@*">
   <xsl:value-of select="."/>
</xsl:template>
```

As shown, the template match value is defined as:

```
text()|@*
```

These characters represent an XPath expression:

- text() is a reference to a function. The text() function is used to obtain the text contents of an element.
- | is a choice indicator, indicating to match either by using the text() function or the @* expression.
- @* is an expression that obtains the value of attributes.

Thus, the expression says to obtain the contents of any text or attribute node. The value-of select="." statement tells the XSLT processor to select these contents and copy them to the output tree. This template is only invoked when you define a template rule that attempts to access the contents of a text or attribute node, and in this case only the contents of the specified node are copied to the node tree.

Understanding Other Built-In Templates

The built-in template for comments and processing instructions is defined as:

```
<xsl:template match="comment()|processing-instruction()" />
```

This is similar to the built-in template for namespaces, which is defined as:

```
<xsl:template match="namespace()" />
```

These built-in templates define no rules for comment, processing-instruction, and namespace nodes. Essentially, this is the same as saying don't do anything. These templates are only invoked when you define template rules that access comment, processing-instruction, or namespace nodes, and then the templates only work to ensure that the nodes are recognized. If you want the contents of these nodes to be extracted, you must define specific template rules to handle this.

Structuring XSLT Stylesheets

XSLT stylesheets are used to transform XML documents into another format. To do this, stylesheets contain rules that match various parts of the input document to a template that specifies how to format that particular part of the document. Every XSLT stylesheet is itself an XML document that contains three basic structures:

- An XSLT declaration that marks the start of the stylesheet.
- An output declaration that sets the output format.
- Template rules containing declarations.

Typically, these structures are applied in the order specified. This means that you start the stylesheet with the XSLT declaration, insert an optional output declaration, and then define template rules containing declarations.

Starting the XSLT Stylesheet

Because an XSLT stylesheet is an XML document, it can start with a standard XML declaration that specifies the XML version, such as:

```
<?xml version="1.0"?>
```

However, the XML declaration isn't required and is omitted in most cases.

The optional XML declaration is followed by the <stylesheet> element, which defines the XSLT version being used and defines the namespace for XSLT definitions. The standard stylesheet declaration for XSLT version 2.0 is:

```
<xsl:stylesheet version="2.0"
  xmlns:xsl="http://www.w3.org/1999/XSL/Transform">
```

This declaration sets the version number and namespace prefix as xsl and points to the Uniform Resource Identifier (URI) *http://www.w3.org/1999/XSL/Transform/*. The closing tag for the stylesheet element is </stylesheet>. This means the basic form of a stylesheet is:

```
<xsl:stylesheet version="2.0"
  xmlns:xsl="http://www.w3.org/1999/XSL/Transform">
...
</xsl:stylesheet>
```

For ease of reference, XSLT stylesheets normally are saved with the .xsl extension. The .xsl extension ensures that the document is easily recognized as containing XSL and that applications, such as Microsoft Internet Explorer, view the document as such.

To define an XSLT stylesheet, follow these steps:

1. Type **<xsl:stylesheet** to declare the namespace prefix as xsl.
2. Specify the XSLT version number using **version="1.0"**, **version="1.1"**, **version="2.0"** or **version="3.0"**.
3. Specify the namespace for the stylesheet by typing **xmlns:xsl="http://www.w3.org/1999/XSL/Transform**.
4. Close the tag by typing **>**.
5. Type a few blank lines where you'll later enter the body of the stylesheet.
6. Type **</xsl:stylesheet>** to complete the stylesheet.

The result should look similar to the following:

```
<xsl:stylesheet version="2.0"
  xmlns:xsl="http://www.w3.org/1999/XSL/Transform">
```

```
...
</xsl:stylesheet>
```

You also could add the namespace for XSL-FO:

```
xmlns:fo=http://www.w3.org/1999/XSL/Format
```

The result would then look similar to the following:

```
<xsl:stylesheet version="2.0"
  xmlns:xsl="http://www.w3.org/1999/XSL/Transform"
  xmlns:fo="http://www.w3.org/1999/XSL/Format">
...
</xsl:stylesheet>
```

Defining the Output Format

You specify the format for output documents using the `output` element. Although this element has no required attributes, it has many optional attributes. These attributes and their uses are discussed in the following sections.

Setting Attributes for the output Element

The primary attribute of the `output` element that you'll use is method, which sets the output method. The XSLT specification defines three possible output methods that processors are required to support:

- **method="xml"** Used when the output contains XML or an XML-based application, such as content formatted with XML-FO or content that uses Scalable Vector Graphics (SVG).
- **method="html"** Used when the output contains standard HTML.
- **method="text"** Used when the output contains text characters. These characters could represent standard text or the source code for a programming language.

> **Note** Because XHTML is an XML-based application, you could set the output method to method="xml" when you want the output document to be formatted as XHTML. You could also set method="html". If you do this, be sure to set attributes that build the appropriate XML and DOCTYPE declarations. For an example, see the section of this chapter entitled "Formatting Output as XML."

The default output method is either XML or HTML, as determined by the contents of the `output`. If the `output` contains text and the root element is named `html` (in any combination of uppercase or lowercase characters), the default output method is HTML. Otherwise, the default output method is XML.

Although XSLT processors are free to implement other output methods, these are the standard output methods. The following example shows how you could set the output method to text:

```
<xsl:stylesheet version="2.0"
  xmlns:xsl="http://www.w3.org/1999/XSL/Transform">

<xsl:output method="text" />
...
</xsl:stylesheet>
```

Table 1-1 provides a summary of the `output` element's attributes. Example procedures using essential attributes with each of the standard output types are discussed in the following sections.

Table 1-1. Attributes of the XSLT output Element

ATTRIBUTE	DESCRIPTION
cdata-section-elements	Lists elements that should be written as CDATA sections in the output. Processor will escape characters as necessary to ensure contents can be output. Used with method="xml".
doctype-	Sets the public identifier to be used in the document

public	type declaration. Used with method="xml" or method="html".
doctype-system	Sets the system identifier to be used in the document type declaration. Used with method="xml" or method="html".
encoding	Defines the character encoding to set in the XML or HTML declaration or the preferred encoding for text. Used with method="xml", method="html" or method="text".
indent	Determines whether the processor can indent the tags in the output document. The value must be yes or no. Processors aren't required to indent. Used with method="xml" or method="html"
media-type	Sets the media type (Multipurpose Internet Mail Extension [MIME] content type) of the output data. Used with method="xml", method="html" or method="text".
method	Sets the output method. Typically, the value is xml, html, or text.
omit-xml-declaration	Determines whether the processor should omit the XML declaration in the output. The value must be yes or no. Used with method="xml".
standalone	Sets the standalone attribute in the XML declaration of the output document. The value must be yes or no. Used with method="xml".
version	Sets the version attribute of the HTML or XML declaration in the output document. Used with method="xml" or method="html".

Formatting Output as XML

XML is one of the two default output formats for XSLT stylesheets. Output is formatted as XML any time the `output` doesn't contain a root element named `html` (in any combination of upper or lowercase characters). If you like, you can explicitly specify that the output should be formatted as XML. Simply set method="xml" in the `output` element of the stylesheet, as shown in this example:

```
<xsl:stylesheet version="2.0"
  xmlns:xsl="http://www.w3.org/1999/XSL/Transform">
```

```
<xsl:output method="xml" />
...
</xsl:stylesheet>
```

When you define the output as XML, you can set attributes that build the output document's XML declaration. The key attributes are: `version`, `standalone`, and `encoding`—`version` sets the XML version being used; `standalone` specifies whether the document is a stand-alone document that doesn't use external files; `encoding` specifies the character encoding of the output document. If you don't specify values for these attributes, the XML declaration is created as:

```
<?xml version="1.0" encoding="UTF-8"?>
```

and the document is considered to be a standalone document. You can modify the default values by setting explicit values. For example, if you wanted the XML declaration to look like this:

```
<?xml version="1.0" encoding="ISO-8859_1" standalone="yes"?>
```

you'd set the attributes of the output element like this:

```
<xsl:output method="xml" version="2.0" encoding="ISO-8859_1"
standalone="yes"/>
```

Any time the output is formatted using an application of XML, such as XML-FO or Scalable Vector Graphics (SVG), you should explicitly set the output method as XML and then define any additional attributes necessary to properly interpret the output document. With SVG, for example, you'll want to set the public and system identifiers so that a DOCTYPE declaration containing these values will be created in the output document. To do this, you set the `doctype-public` and `doctype-system` attributes of the `output` element. With SVG, the standard values for these attributes are "-//W3C//DTD SVG 1.1//EN" and "http://www.w3.org/Graphics/SVG/1.1/DTD/svg11.dtd", respectively.

Note The value EN in the PUBLIC URI for SVG is the two-letter language code for U.S. English. If the document isn't formatted in U.S. English, you must change the language code to the appropriate value.

The following example shows how you could set the doctype-public and doctype-system attributes in a stylesheet:

```
<?xml version="1.0"?>
<xsl:stylesheet version="3.0"
  xmlns:xsl="http://www.w3.org/1999/XSL/Transform">

  <xsl:output method="xml"
   doctype-public="-//W3C//DTD SVG 1.1//EN"
   doctype-system=
"http://www.w3.org/Graphics/SVG/1.1/DTD/svg11.dtd"/>

 <xsl:template match="/">
  <svg>
  ...
  </svg>
 </xsl:template>

</xsl:stylesheet>
```

In the output document these values would be defined like this:

```
<?xml version="1.0" encoding="UTF-8"?>
<!DOCTYPE svg PUBLIC "-//W3C//DTD SVG 1.1//EN"
"http://www.w3.org/Graphics/SVG/1.1/DTD/svg11.dtd">
<svg>
...
</svg>
```

You can also use the doctype-public and doctype-system attributes when you want to format output as XHTML. With XHTML, these attributes are set to "-//W3C//DTD XHTML 2.0 Strict//EN" and "http://www.w3.org/TR/xhtml2/DTD/xhtml2-strict.dtd", respectively in most cases. This means a typical stylesheet for XHTML looks like this:

```
<?xml version="1.0"?>
<xsl:stylesheet version="3.0"
  xmlns:xsl="http://www.w3.org/1999/XSL/Transform">

  <xsl:output method="xml"
   doctype-public="-//W3C//DTD XHTML 2.0 Strict//EN"
   doctype-system="http://www.w3.org/TR/xhtml2/DTD/xhtml2-
strict.dtd"/>

 <xsl:template match="/">
  <html>
  ...
  </html>
 </xsl:template>

</xsl:stylesheet>
```

and these values appear in the output document like this:

```
<?xml version="1.0" encoding="UTF-8"?>
<!DOCTYPE svg PUBLIC "-//W3C//DTD XHTML 2.0 Strict//EN"
"http://www.w3.org/TR/xhtml2/DTD/xhtml2-strict.dtd ">
<html>
...
</html>
```

Note As before, the value EN in the PUBLIC URI is the two-letter language code for U.S. English. If the document isn't formatted in U.S. English, you must change the language code to the appropriate value. The PUBLIC and SYSTEM URIs also reference the strict version of the XHTML 2.0 DTD. References to transitional and frameset are also possible.

Now that you've seen basic examples, lets take a more detailed look at the conversion process. The following example defines an XSLT stylesheet that formats the example XML document used earlier in the chapter using XML-FO:

```
<?xml version="1.0"?>
<xsl:stylesheet version="3.0"
  xmlns:xsl="http://www.w3.org/1999/XSL/Transform"
  xmlns:fo="http://www.w3.org/1999/XSL/Format">

 <xsl:output method="xml"/>

 <xsl:template match="/">
  <fo:root xmlns:fo="http://www.w3.org/1999/XSL/Format">
   <fo:layout-master-set>
    <fo:simple-page-master margin-right="50pt" margin-
left="50pt"
     page-height="11in" page-width="8.5in"
     margin-bottom="35pt" margin-top="35pt" master-
name="main">
     <fo:region-before extent="25pt"/>
     <fo:region-body margin-top="50pt" margin-bottom="50pt"/>
     <fo:region-after extent="25pt"/>
    </fo:simple-page-master>
    <fo:page-sequence-master master-name="standard">
     <fo:repeatable-page-master-alternatives>
      <fo:conditional-page-master-reference
          master-name="main" odd-or-even="any"/>
     </fo:repeatable-page-master-alternatives>
    </fo:page-sequence-master>
   </fo:layout-master-set>

   <fo:page-sequence master-name="standard">
    <fo:flow flow-name="xsl-region-body">
```

```
      <xsl:apply-templates select="document"/>
     </fo:flow>
    </fo:page-sequence>
   </fo:root>
  </xsl:template>

  <xsl:template match="document">
   <fo:block line-height="16pt" font-size="12pt" text-
align="left">
    <xsl:value-of select="."/>
   </fo:block>
  </xsl:template>

</xsl:stylesheet>
```

Here, the stylesheet applies formatting to the document using XML-FO. The formatting entries set the page size to 8 ½" x 11"; define a master page layout with margins for the top, bottom, left, and right sides of the page; and then define the formatting for the body of the page. Using an XSLT processor, we could use this stylesheet to transform the sample.xml document defined earlier in the chapter.

The output of the transformation process is the following XML document containing formatted objects:

```
<?xml version="1.0" encoding="UTF-8"?>
<fo:root xmlns:fo="http://www.w3.org/1999/XSL/Format">
 <fo:layout-master-set>
  <fo:simple-page-master margin-right="50pt" margin-
left="50pt"
   page-height="11in" page-width="8.5in"
   margin-bottom="35pt" margin-top="35pt" master-name="main">
   <fo:region-before extent="25pt"/>
   <fo:region-body margin-top="50pt" margin-bottom="50pt"/>
   <fo:region-after extent="25pt"/>
  </fo:simple-page-master>
  <fo:page-sequence-master master-name="standard">
   <fo:repeatable-page-master-alternatives>
    <fo:conditional-page-master-reference
```

```
        master-name="main" odd-or-even="any"/>
    </fo:repeatable-page-master-alternatives>
   </fo:page-sequence-master>
  </fo:layout-master-set>

  <fo:page-sequence master-name="standard">
   <fo:flow flow-name="xsl-region-body">
     <fo:block line-height="16pt" font-size="12pt" text-
align="left">
     XSLT is a powerful transformation language.
     </fo:block>
   </fo:flow>
  </fo:page-sequence>
</fo:root>
```

You can easily convert documents that use XML-FO to other document formats, such as Adobe's PDF. Once you convert the document to PDF, you could view it in Adobe Acrobat.

Real World I hope you're starting to see the true power of XSLT as a document transformation powerhouse. Imagine implementing automated transformations for an e-commerce Web site. Here, you could extract data formatted as XML directly from a database and then use XSLT to transform the data into a document in any desired output format.

Formatting Output as HTML

HTML is the other default output format for XSLT stylesheets. Output is formatted as HTML any time the output contains text and has a root element named html (in any combination of upper or lowercase characters). If you like, you can explicitly specify that the output should be formatted as HTML. Simply set method="html" in the stylesheet, as shown in this example:

```
<xsl:stylesheet version="2.0"
```

```
  xmlns:xsl="http://www.w3.org/1999/XSL/Transform">

  <xsl:output method="html"/>

  <xsl:template match="/">
    <xsl:apply-templates select="document"/>
  </xsl:template>

  <xsl:template match="document">
    <html>
      <body>
        <p>
          <xsl:value-of select="."/>
        </p>
      </body>
    </html>
  </xsl:template>

</xsl:stylesheet>
```

You saw this example earlier in the chapter used to convert the sample XML document to HTML. Because XSLT is so versatile, there are always additional ways to perform tasks. To create the same output document, you could have also used the following XSLT template:

```
<xsl:stylesheet version="2.0"
  xmlns:xsl="http://www.w3.org/1999/XSL/Transform">

  <xsl:output method="html"/>

  <xsl:template match="/">
    <html>
      <body>
        <xsl:apply-templates select="document"/>
      </body>
    </html>
  </xsl:template>
```

```
  <xsl:template match="document">
        <p>
          <xsl:value-of select="."/>
        </p>
  </xsl:template>

</xsl:stylesheet>
```

The subtle difference between this template and the previous template is that the `html` and body elements are built in the root template and only the contents of the `document` element are evaluated in the second template. This subtle change lets you easily handle the case where there are multiple `document` elements and you want to output a properly formatted document. For example, if you rewrote the sample document to contain multiple `document` elements like this:

```
<?xml version="1.0"?>
<definitions>
 <document>
  XML is a language for describing other languages.
 </document>
 <document>
  XSLT is a powerful transformation language.
 </document>
</definitions>
```

the modified stylesheet would ensure that the output document was formatted like this:

```
<html>
<body>
<p>
  XML is a language for describing other languages.
</p>
<p>
  XSLT is a powerful transformation language.
</p>
</body>
</html>
```

Without this change, we'd end up with a document that was incorrectly formatted and looked like this:

```
<html>
<body>
<p>
  XML is a language for describing other languages.
</p>
</body>
</html>
<html>
<body>
<p>
  XSLT is a powerful transformation language.
</p>
</body>
</html>
```

When you use HTML, you'll often want to associate the output with a cascading style sheet or make direct style assignments. If you've worked with HTML and CSS before, defining style for an output document formatted as HTML is easy. Consider the following example output document that has two styles for paragraph tags defined:

```
<html>
  <head>
  <title>Using Classes in Style Sheets</title>
  <style type="text/css">
    <!--
    p.styleA  {font: 45pt Times; color: brown}
    p.styleB  {font: 30pt Arial; color: blue}
    -->
  </style>
  </head>
  <body>
    <p class="styleA"> This is a paragraph in styleA</p>
    <p class="styleB"> This is a paragraph in styleB</p>
  <body>
```

```
</html>
```

To transform an XML document into an HTML that looks like this, you'd define the XSLT stylesheet like this:

```
<xsl:stylesheet version="2.0"
  xmlns:xsl="http://www.w3.org/1999/XSL/Transform">

  <xsl:output method="html"/>

  <xsl:template match="/">
    <html>
      <head>
        <title>Using Classes in Style Sheets</title>
        <style type="text/css">
          <xsl:comment>
           p.styleA  {font: 45pt Times; color: brown}
           p.styleB  {font: 30pt Arial; color: blue}
          </xsl:comment>
        </style>
      </head>
      <body>
          <xsl:apply-templates
select="definitions/document1"/>
          <xsl:apply-templates
select="definitions/document2"/>
      </body>
    </html>
  </xsl:template>

  <xsl:template match="document1">
        <p class="styleA">
          <xsl:value-of select="."/>
        </p>
  </xsl:template>

  <xsl:template match="document2">
        <p class="styleB">
```

```
        <xsl:value-of select="."/>
      </p>
  </xsl:template>

</xsl:stylesheet>
```

In this example, note that the HTML comment tags (<!-- and -->) are replaced with the `xsl:comment` tags (<xsl:comment> and </xsl:comment>) and that template matches are for elements named `document1` and `document2`, respectively. `document1` and `document2` are arbitrary names that represent elements in the input document that you want to format with either styleA or styleB. You could replace these arbitrary names with the names of any valid elements from the input document.

Although you can make internal style assignments, cascading style sheets are more typically defined externally. In HTML, you specify the location of an external cascading style sheet using the link element in the form:

```
<link rel="stylesheet" type="text/css" href="mystyles.css">
```

In the XSLT stylesheet that defines your output HTML document, you could insert this `link` element directly with one noteworthy exception. You'd have to define the linked stylesheet as an empty element, such as:

```
<link rel="stylesheet" type="text/css" href="mystyles.css" />
```

You could then insert the `link` element directly into the XSLT stylesheet as shown in this example:

```
<xsl:stylesheet version="2.0"
  xmlns:xsl="http://www.w3.org/1999/XSL/Transform">

  <xsl:output method="html"/>

  <xsl:template match="/">
    <html>
      <head>
        <link rel="stylesheet" type="text/css"
href="mystyles.css" />
```

```
      </head>
      <body>
        <xsl:apply-templates select="document"/>
      </body>
    </html>
  </xsl:template>

  <xsl:template match="document">
        <p>
          <xsl:value-of select="."/>
        </p>
  </xsl:template>

</xsl:stylesheet>
```

Formatting Output as Text or Code

Whenever you want to format the output document as text or program source code, you specify the output format as method="text". Afterward, you insert the literal text or source code into `xsl:text` elements. Here's a basic example of an XSLT stylesheet that's used to output text:

```
<xsl:stylesheet version="2.0"
  xmlns:xsl="http://www.w3.org/1999/XSL/Transform">

  <xsl:output method="html"/>

  <xsl:template match="/">
    <xsl:apply-templates select="document"/>
  </xsl:template>

  <xsl:template match="document">
    <xsl:text>
The contents of the document element are:
    </xsl:text>
    <xsl:value-of select="."/>
    <xsl:text>
.
```

```
    </xsl:text>
  </xsl:template>

</xsl:stylesheet>
```

If the input XML document for this stylesheet looked like this:

```
<?xml version="1.0"?>
<document>
XSLT, XML, XSL-FO
</document>
```

the output after transformation would look like this:

```
The contents of the document element are: XSLT, XML, XSL-FO.
```

With source code, the trick is to ensure that you apply templates and switch to literal text in the appropriate locations to get the exact output you desire. Consider the following Java source:

```
class hello {
  public static void main(String[] args) {
    System.out.println("Hello, " + args[0] + "!");
  }
}
```

This short snippet of code writes a string to the standard output. If the program is run with the command:

```
java Hello William
```

the output string is:

```
Hello, William!
```

You could rewrite this program within an XSLT stylesheet so that the program gets its output argument from the contents of a specific element. For example, if your XML document was defined as:

```
<?xml version="1.0"?>
<name>
Bob
</name>
```

an XSLT stylesheet that used the document with the previous Java source code would look like this:

```
<?xml version="1.0"?>
<xsl:stylesheet version="3.0"
  xmlns:xsl="http://www.w3.org/1999/XSL/Transform">

  <xsl:output method="text"/>

  <xsl:template match="/">
    <xsl:text>
      class hello {
        public static void main(String[] args) {
    </xsl:text>
    <xsl:apply-templates select="name"/>
    <xsl:text>
        }
      }
    </xsl:text>
  </xsl:template>

  <xsl:template match="name">
    <xsl:text>System.out.println("Hello, </xsl:text>
    <xsl:value-of select="."/>
    <xsl:text>!");</xsl:text>
  </xsl:template>

</xsl:stylesheet>
```

Based on the contents of the input document, the output after transformation is:

```
class hello {
  public static void main(String[] args) {
```

```
      System.out.println("Hello, Bob!");
    }
}
```

> **Note** More precisely, the output would contain a few extra spaces because of how the name tag is defined and used in the template. To get rid of these extra spaces, you could replace `value of select="."` with `value of select="normalize-space()"`. I'll talk about this and other available functions in upcoming chapters.

Setting the Output Format

As you've seen, you can transform XML documents in many ways using XSLT. Regardless of which output format you choose, the basic steps you follow to set the output format are the same. These steps are:

1. After the begin stylesheet element, type **<xsl:output**.
2. If you want to set a specific output method other than the default, type **method="*format*"**, where *format* sets the output format. The standard values are xml, html, and text.
3. Specify other attributes for the output element as necessary. For example, if you wanted to encode the document using ISO 8859 Latin 1, you'd set **encoding="ISO-8859_1"**.
4. Type **/>** to complete the output element.

The result should look similar to the following:

```
<xsl:output method="format" attrib1="value" attrib2="value"
attribN="value"/>
```

Defining Template Rules and Declarations

The processes of defining template rules and making template declarations go hand in hand. Whenever you define a template rule, you use a set of matching criteria to determine which template should be processed. The contents of the template rule are the individual declarations that you want to make. (Throughout this text, I refer to the template rule and the declarations it contains as a template).

The following sections examine basic techniques you can use to define template rules and declarations. More advanced techniques are covered in subsequent chapters.

Creating the Root Template

As previously explained in this chapter, all templates are processed recursively, starting with the root template. This means that the root template is at the top of the execution tree and all other templates are processed after the root template. The basic format of a template rule that matches the root node is:

```
<xsl:template match="/">
...
</xsl:template>
```

Although you can enter templates in any order in the XSLT stylesheet, you'll usually want the root template to be at the top of the stylesheet and other templates to follow. With this in mind, the steps you follow to create the root template are

1. After you've defined the stylesheet's start tag and output method, type **<xsl:template**.
2. Type **match="/">** to indicate that the template rule should match the root node and complete the xsl:template element.
3. Create template rules for other nodes in the input document as specified in the next section of this chapter, which is titled "Creating and Applying Template Rules."
4. Type **</xsl:template>** to complete the template.

Your stylesheet should now look similar to this:

```
<xsl:stylesheet version="2.0"
  xmlns:xsl="http://www.w3.org/1999/XSL/Transform">

  <xsl:output method="html"/>
```

```
  <xsl:template match="/">
  ...
  </xsl:template>

</xsl:stylesheet>
```

Creating and Applying Template Rules

Template rules describe how a particular section of a document should be output. The basic format of a template rule is:

```
<xsl:template match="pattern">
...
</xsl:template>
```

where *pattern* identifies the sections of the document to which the template should be applied. The inner section of the template rule determines what happens when a match is found. To ensure that another template rule is processed, you must use the `apply-templates` element to select the node or nodes that you want to process. The basic format of the `apply-templates` element is:

```
<xsl:apply-templates select="expression"/>
```

where *expression* is an XPath expression that identifies the nodes whose templates should be applied.

To perform some other type of processing, you must specify the appropriate actions. For example, to display the value of nodes that match the template rule, you could use the `xsl:value-of` element as discussed in the next section of this chapter, which is titled "Outputting the Contents of Nodes."

Template rules are recursively processed starting with the template rule for the root node. To take advantage of recursion, you typically apply templates for top-level nodes in the root template, the next level nodes inside the templates for top-level nodes, and so on. For example, if the input document looked like this:

```
<?xml version="1.0"?>
<root>
```

```
  <elementA id="s1">
   <elementB>B1's contents
   </elementB>
   <elementC>C1's contents
   </elementC>
   <elementD>D1's contents
   </elementD>
  <elementA>

  <elementA id="s2">
   <elementB>B2's contents
   </elementB>
   <elementC>C2's contents
   </elementC>
   <elementD>D2's contents
   </elementD>
  <elementA>
</root>
```

you might define the set of template rules that processes these elements as:

```
<xsl:template match="/">
  <xsl:apply-templates select="elementA"/>
</xsl:template>

<xsl:template match="elementA">
  <xsl:apply-templates select="elementB"/>
  <xsl:apply-templates select="elementC"/>
  <xsl:apply-templates select="elementD"/>
</xsl:template>

<xsl:template match="elementB">
...
</xsl:template>

<xsl:template match="elementC">
...
</xsl:template>
```

```
<xsl:template match="elementD">
...
</xsl:template>
```

This would ensure that nodes are processed recursively in the following order:

> root → elementA id="s1" → elementB1 → elementC1 → elementD1 → elementA id="s2" → elementB2 → elementC2 → elementD2

To create a template rule that applies another template, follow these steps:

1. After you've defined the stylesheet's start tag and output method, type **<xsl:template match="*pattern*">**, where *pattern* identifies the sections of the document to which the template should be applied.
2. Type **<xsl:apply-templates select="*expression*"/>**, where *expression* identifies the nodes whose templates should be applied. Repeat this step to apply other template rules.
3. Type **</xsl:template>** to complete the template.

The result should look similar to the following:

```
<xsl:template match="pattern">
  <xsl:apply-templates select="expression1"/>
  <xsl:apply-templates select="expression2"/>
  ...
  <xsl:apply-templates select="expressionN"/>
</xsl:template>
```

Outputting the Contents of Nodes

After you define template rules for the root element and top-level elements, you'll want to define rules that apply to low-level elements that contain text. In most cases you'll want to display the value of this text in the output document. As shown in previous examples in this chapter, you can use the `xsl:value-of` element to display the contents of a particular node. The basic format of this element is:

```
<xsl:value-of select="expression" />
```

where *expression* identifies the node or nodes whose content should be output at the current position in the output document.

In most of the previous examples in this chapter, I've used the value . to specify that the contents of the current node should be displayed. Although you can reference the current node, you can reference any other node in the document as well. For example, you can reference the child node of the current node simply by entering the name of the child node. These values are XPath expressions called location paths, which you'll learn about in Chapter 2.

Following this discussion, you could output the contents of the current node or a child node of the current node by following these steps:

1. Within the template rule that you want to work with, type **<xsl:value-of** to begin the declaration.
2. Type **select="."/>** to specify the current node's contents or type **select="*name*"/>** to specify that the contents of the named child element of the current element should be output.

The result should be similar to the following.

```
<xsl:template match="pattern">
  <xsl:value-of select="." />
</xsl:template>
```

Chapter 2. XPath Operators & Expressions

XSL Transformations (XSLT) uses XML Path (XPath) to access and refer to parts of an input document. XPath locates various document structures by representing those structures as node trees that can be navigated using location paths. The location paths have a very specific syntax that includes operators and expressions used to locate parts of a document according to the type of structure they represent. The seven basic structures that location paths allow you to access are

- **Root nodes** Represent the root element in XML documents
- **Element nodes** Represent all elements in XML documents, including root nodes
- **Attribute nodes** Represent attributes in XML documents, including default and inherited attributes (but excluding xmlns attributes)
- **Text nodes** Represent the text contents of elements including any CDATA sections that elements might contain
- **Comment nodes** Represent the text components of comments that are inserted into XML documents
- **Processing instruction nodes** Represent processing instructions in XML documents by name and string value
- **Namespace nodes** Represent namespaces declared in XSLT stylesheets as defined in xmlns attributes

As you learned in the previous chapter, "XSL Transformations and Formatting," you can refer to these node types as part of match and select expressions for various XSLT elements. This allows you to create template rules that match various node types and then to specify the transformations that should be applied to those node types. The catch is that the only part of an XSLT stylesheet that's processed automatically is the template rule for a root node, which is referred to by the location path /. Because of this, you use template rules for root nodes to start the transformation process and typically design your XSLT stylesheets to use recursion to extract information from input documents.

Understanding Location Paths

Recursion is a powerful aspect of XSLT. It allows you to locate various structures according to their context in a document. Essentially, you work from the root context in a document to the top-level nodes and then you explore successive levels of nodes associated with each top-level node until you've examined all the structures in a document that you want to work with.

The / representing the root node is only one of the many XPath expressions you can use. Each expression follows a specific syntax and can make use of various operators to locate specific types of nodes. You can access nodes using location paths that are context-specific as well as by using paths that are context-free.

The basic difference between context-specific and context-free location paths has to do with which nodes are located. With context-specific location paths, nodes are evaluated according to the context in which they appear, allowing you to match a node relative to its location in a document. With context-free location paths, nodes are evaluated directly and outside of a specific context, allowing you to locate nodes by specifying their absolute location without regard to the current context. To better understand the impact of context, consider the following XML document:

```
<?xml version="1.0" ?>
<inventory>
   <item tracking_number="459323" manufacturer="Not listed">
      <item_type>Fiberglass Prehung Entry Door</item_type>
      <description>6-panel left-hand inswing entry door,
primed, white</description>
   </item>
   <item tracking_number="459789" manufacturer="Not listed">
      <item_type>Steel Prehung Entry Door</item_type>
      <description>4-panel left-hand inswing entry door,
primed, black, steel</description>
   </item>
</inventory>
```

A basic node tree representing the elements of this document could look like this:

```
-inventory
   -item
      -item_type
      -description
   -item
      -item_type
      -description
```

Essentially, this node tree representation says that the root element, `inventory`, has two `item` elements as its only children. The `item` elements in turn have two child elements called `item_type` and `description`.

You could locate these elements using many techniques. The following example uses recursion to work with elements in a context-specific manner:

```
<xsl:template match="/">
    <html>
      <body>
        <xsl:apply-templates select="inventory/item"/>
      </body>
    </html>
</xsl:template>

<xsl:template match="item">
  <xsl:apply-templates select="item_type"/>
  <xsl:apply-templates select="description"/>
</xsl:template>

<xsl:template match="item_type">
<h1>
   <xsl:value-of select="."/>
</h1>
</xsl:template>

<xsl:template match="description">
<p>
   <xsl:value-of select="."/>
```

```
</p>
</xsl:template>
```

Real World Namespaces are tracked separately by XSLT processors using namespace nodes. Every root, element, and attribute node defined in a document can have a namespace associated with it. If so, you must reference the qualified name in your XSLT stylesheets. For example, if the namespace for the inventory document were inv, you'd reference `inv:item`, `inv:item_type`, and `inv:description` rather than `item`, `item_type`, and `description`, respectively.

Based on this XSLT stylesheet, the inventory document is processed in the following order:

root → item1 → item_type → description → item2 → item_type → description

and the output document would look like this:

```
<html>
<body>
<h1>Fiberglass Prehung Entry Door</h1>
<p>6-panel left-hand inswing entry door, primed, white</p>
<h1>Steel Prehung Entry Door</h1>
<p>4-panel left-hand inswing entry door, primed, black,
steel</p>
</body>
</html>
```

When you work with the current context, XPath expressions are evaluated relative to the context node. Because expressions can match multiple nodes, the XSLT processor maintains a pointer of sorts that tracks the context position and the context size. The context position refers to the position of the node currently being processed. The context size refers to the number of nodes selected by the current expression. Together, the context position and context size allow the XSLT processor to navigate the node tree in terms of the current context.

If the inventory document contained a single `item` element whose contents we wanted to work with directly, such as:

```
<?xml version="1.0" ?>
<inventory>
   <summary>Inventory Summary for 12 - 15 - 02</summary>
   <item tracking_number="459323" manufacturer="Not listed">
      <item_type>Fiberglass Prehung Entry Door</item_type>
      <description>6-panel left-hand inswing entry door,
primed, white</description>
   </item>
   <details>No details available.</details>
</inventory>
```

we could process the item element directly rather than in terms of the current context. Here's an example:

```
<xsl:template match="/">
    <html>
      <body>
        <h1>
          <xsl:apply-templates
select="/inventory/item/item_type"/>
        </h1>


         <p>
           <xsl:apply-templates
select="/inventory/item/description"/>
         </p>


      </body>
    </html>
</xsl:template>
```

In this example you specify the elements you want to work with using an absolute path. Absolute paths differ from relative paths in that they're always located in terms of the root element rather than in terms of the current context. The first apply-templates declaration:

```
<xsl:apply-templates select="/inventory/item/item_type"/>
```

specifies that there's a root element called `inventory` that contains an `item` element that in turn has an `item_type` element associated with it. This expression tells the XSLT processor to return all nodes that have this absolute path. In the previous document, this would mean that the processor would return the node defined as follows:

```
<item_type>Fiberglass Prehung Entry Door</item_type>
```

The second apply-templates declaration:

```
<xsl:apply-templates select="/inventory/item/description"/>
```

specifies that there's a root element called `inventory` that contains an `item` element that in turn has a `description` element associated with it. This expression tells the XSLT processor to return all nodes that have this absolute path. In the previous document, this would mean that the processor would return the node defined as follows:

```
<description>6-panel left-hand inswing entry door, primed,
white</description>
```

Based on this, the resulting output document would look like this:

```
<html>
<body>
<h1>Fiberglass Prehung Entry Door</h1>
<p>6-panel left-hand inswing entry door, primed, white</p>
</body>
</html>
```

Unfortunately, these XSLT expressions wouldn't work the way you intended if the document contained multiple items subsets. Remember, the processor returns all matching nodes with the specified absolute path. To allow for the case where multiple items were in the inventory document and you wanted to use absolute paths, you'd have to modify the XSLT stylesheet. The following example shows one way you could do this:

```
<xsl:template match="/">
    <html>
      <body>
        <h1>Inventory Item Summary</h1>
        <xsl:apply-templates
select="/inventory/item/item_type"/>
        <h1>Description Summary</h1>
        <xsl:apply-templates
select="/inventory/item/description"/>
      </body>
    </html>
</xsl:template>

<xsl:template match="/inventory/item/item_type">
  <p>
    <xsl:value-of select="."/>
  </p>
</xsl:template>

<xsl:template match="/inventory/item/description">
  <p>
    <xsl:value-of select="."/>
  </p>
</xsl:template>
```

With the original inventory document defined as:

```
<?xml version="1.0" ?>
<inventory>
   <item tracking_number="459323" manufacturer="Not listed">
      <item_type>Fiberglass Prehung Entry Door</item_type>
      <description>6-panel left-hand inswing entry door,
primed, white</description>
   </item>
   <item tracking_number="459789" manufacturer="Not listed">
```

```
        <item_type>Steel Prehung Entry Door</item_type>
        <description>4-panel left-hand inswing entry door,
primed, black, steel</description>
    </item>
</inventory>
```

the output is now:

```
<html>
<body>
<h1>Inventory Item Summary</h1>
<p>Fiberglass Prehung Entry Door</p>
<p>Steel Prehung Entry Door</p>
<h1>Description Summary</h1>
<p>6-panel left-hand inswing entry door, primed, white</p>
<p>4-panel left-hand inswing entry door, primed, black,
steel</p>
</body>
</html>
```

As you can see from the output, the `item_type` values are listed first, followed by a list of `description` values. This output would be useful if you wanted to list the contents of various elements in separate lists. However, the output isn't optimal in this case. Here, you might want to use relative paths and rework the XSLT stylesheet accordingly.

Understanding XPath Operators and Datatypes

In this chapter and the previous one, you've seen various operators, such as . and /, used in examples. XPath defines many other operators that you can used in expressions to locate nodes. In this section I've divided these operators into three broad categories to provide a resource summary of the various operators that are available.

Table 2-1 summarizes standard XPath operators. These operators are the ones you'll use most often with XSLT and XPath.

Table 2-1. XPath Standard Operators

OPERATOR	DESCRIPTION
/	A path separator used to indicate successive levels of the node tree hierarchy. If used at the beginning of an expression, it represents the root node.
.	Refers to the current context node.
..	Refers to the parent of the current context node.
@	Indicates an attribute reference.
*	A wildcard that selects any node of the principal node type; with element nodes, this would select or match any element node in the current context.
@*	A wildcard that selects or matches any attribute node in the current context.
node()	Selects all nodes in the current context regardless of type. (Technically, this is type of a node test that's used as a wildcard.)
//	Allows you to skip levels in the hierarchy; indicates that zero or more elements may occur between the slashes.
[]	Predicate operator used in predicate expressions to filter a group of nodes.
|	Selects either match in a series, such as match="a|b|c" to match a, b, and c elements.
$	Variable operator used to indicate variable names.

In addition to defining standard operators, XPath defines a set of mathematical and Boolean operators. These operators are summarized in Table 2-2. Although mathematical operators evaluate expressions to specific values, Boolean operators evaluate expressions as Booleans (either true or false). Booleans are only one of the five data types that can be used with XPath. The other datatypes are

- **node-set** Represents a set of nodes. Node sets can be empty or they can contain any number of nodes.

- **result tree fragment** A temporary tree that holds the value of a result or the value of variable assignment.
- **number** Represents a floating-point number. All floating-point numbers comply with IEEE 754 (which is the same standard used with float and double datatypes used by XML Schema). As with XML Schema, XPath and XSLT floating-point values have five special values: 0 (referred to as positive zero), -0 (referred to as negative zero), INF (referred to as positive infinity), -INF (referred to as negative infinity), and NaN (referred to as not-a-number).
- **string** Represents a sequence of zero or more characters as defined in the XML specification.

Table 2-2. XPath Arithmetic Operators

OPERATOR	DESCRIPTION
*	Multiplication; multiplies one number by another.
div	Division; performs floating-point division on two numbers.
mod	Modulus; returns the floating-point remainder of dividing one number by another.
+	Addition; adds one number to another.
-	Subtraction; subtracts one number from another.
=	Equality; tests whether two expressions are equal.
<	Less than; tests whether the first expression is less than the second.
>	Greater than; tests whether the first expression is greater than the second.
<=	Less than or equals; tests whether the first expression is less than or equal to the second.
>=	Greater than or equals; tests whether the first expression is greater than or equal to the second.
!=	Not equal; tests whether the two expressions aren't equal.
and	Logical And; tests whether the first and the second expression are true. Both expressions must be true for the logical And to evaluate to true.

or	Logical Or; tests whether one of two expressions is true. Only one expression must be true for the logical Or to evaluate to true.

Another type of operator XPath defines is an axis. An axis is an operator keyword that acts as a location designator. You use axes to make unabbreviated XPath references. Axes are useful when you want to use advanced techniques to locate ancestor, descendent, and sibling nodes, but they're too complex for most other uses. Table 2-3 provides a summary of the axes that are available.

Table 2-3. XPath Axes

AXIS TYPE	DESCRIPTION
ancestor	Contains the parent of the context node, the parent's parent, and so on up to the root node (unless, of course, the context node is the root node). Usage: ancestor::node, such as ancestor::item
ancestor-or-self	Contains context node, the parent of the context node, the parent's parent, and so on up to the root node. Usage: ancestor-or-self::node, such as ancestor-or-self::item
attribute	Contains the attributes of the context node Usage: attribute::type or @type
child	Contains the children of the context node. Usage: child::node/child::node, such as child::item/child::item_type.
descendant	Contains the children of the context node, the children's children, and so on to the lowest possible level (unless, of course, the context node is the lowest child node). Usage: descendant::node, such as descendant::item
descendant-or-self	Contains context node, the children of the context node, the children's children, and so on to the lowest possible level. Usage:

	descendant-or-self::node, such as descendant-or-self::item
following	Contains all nodes that appear after the context node in the document except descendants, attribute nodes, and namespace nodes. Usage: following::node, such as following::item
following-sibling	Contains all following siblings of the context node (meaning all nodes that have the same parent as the context node and are after the context node in the current node set). Usage: following-sibling::node, such as following-sibling::item
namespace	Contains all namespace nodes in the context node. If the context node isn't an element node, the axis is empty. Usage: namespace::node, such as namespace::item
parent	Contains the parent of the context node. Usage: parent::node, such as parent::item
preceding	Contains all nodes that appear before the context node in the document except ancestors, attribute nodes, and namespace nodes. Usage: preceding::node, such as preceding::item
preceding-sibling	Contains all preceding siblings of the context node (meaning all nodes that have the same parent as the context node and are before the context node in current node set). Usage: preceding-sibling::node, such as preceding-sibling::item
self	Contains the context node itself. Usage: self::* or .

Using Relative XPath Expressions with Elements

Relative and absolute XPath expressions are similar to Uniform Resource Locators (URLs) used in hypertext references in the way they're used and structured. With relative XPath expressions, you reference locations relative to the current context that the XSLT processor is working with. Relative expressions refer to:

- The current context node using a single period (.)
- A parent of the current node using a double period (..)
- A child of the current node by referencing its name directly
- A named sibling of the current node by referencing ../name
- Nodes in other levels of the hierarchy by referencing their relative path from the current context

Techniques for working with these context-specific expressions are discussed in the following sections.

Referencing the Current Context Node

When you work with the current context, other XPath locations can be referenced relative to the current position. The XPath expression you use to reference the current node itself is a single period (.).

Essentially, the single period (.) says to use the current context node. In the following example, the contents of the current node are selected and output:

```
<xsl:template match="element">
  <html>
    <body>
      <p>
        <xsl:value-of select="."/>
      </p>
    </body>
  </html>
</xsl:template>
```

Following this, if you're currently processing the node that you want to use in a select statement, you can refer to the current node by completing these steps:

1. Type a single period, as in <xsl:value-of select="."/>.
2. Alternatively, specify a predicate expression that selects a subset of the current node, as discussed in the section of this chapter entitled "Filtering To Match Nodes."

Referencing a Parent Node

You can reference the parent of the current context node using a double period (..), such as:

```
<xsl:value-of select=".."/>
```

Essentially, the double period (..) tells XPath to go up one level in the node tree hierarchy. For example, if the current context is processing the `item_type` elements based on this input document:

```
<?xml version="1.0" ?>
<inventory>
   <item tracking_number="459323" manufacturer="Not listed">
      <item_type>Fiberglass Prehung Entry Door</item_type>
      <description>6-panel left-hand inswing entry door,
primed, white</description>
   </item>
   <item tracking_number="459789" manufacturer="Not listed">
      <item_type>Steel Prehung Entry Door</item_type>
      <description>4-panel left-hand inswing entry door,
primed, black, steel</description>
   </item>
</inventory>
```

the parent elements referenced by .. are the `item` elements.

You can also reference the parent of a parent node. For example, if you were working with the description element and wanted to access the `inventory` element (which is the parent of the parent element item), you could extend the parent reference so that it went two levels up the tree using the value:

```
../..
```

Tip This technique can be extended as far as necessary. If you need to go three levels up the node tree, you'd use ../../.., for four levels up the tree you'd use ../../../.., and so on.

You can select the parents of the current node by following these steps:

1. Type **..** to select the parent of the current context node.
2. Optionally, type **/..** to specify a parent of the parent node. Repeat this step to go farther up the hierarchy.

The result should look similar to the following:

```
<xsl:value-of select="../.."/>
```

Referencing Siblings Relative to the Current Context

Relative XPath expressions also allow you to locate nodes at the same level as the current context node. To do this, you reference the parent using double periods (..), enter a slash (/), and then specify the name of the sibling that you want to work with. For example, if you were working with the `item_type` element defined in the following inventory document:

```
<?xml version="1.0" ?>
<inventory>
   <item tracking_number="459323" manufacturer="Not listed">
      <item_type>Fiberglass Prehung Entry Door</item_type>
      <description>6-panel left-hand inswing entry door,
primed, white</description>
   </item>
   <item tracking_number="459789" manufacturer="Not listed">
      <item_type>Steel Prehung Entry Door</item_type>
```

```
        <description>4-panel left-hand inswing entry door,
primed, black, steel</description>
    </item>
    <summary>No summary available</summary>
</inventory>
```

you could reference the `description` element at the same level of the hierarchy using the relative path:

```
../description
```

You can select siblings of the current node by following these steps:

1. Type ***../sibling***, where sibling is the name of node that's at the same level of the node tree as the current node, as in <xsl:value-of select="../item"/>.
2. Alternatively, specify a child node of a sibling by typing ***../sibling/child***, such as <xsl:value-of select="../item/item_type"/>.

Referencing Child Nodes

You can access child nodes of the current context node by referencing the name of the child node. The following example matches all `item_type` elements that are child nodes of the current context node:

```
<xsl:value-of select="item_type"/>
```

Essentially, the direct name reference tells XPath to go to the next lower level in the node tree hierarchy. For example, if the current context is processing `item` elements based on this input document:

```
<?xml version="1.0" ?>
<inventory>
    <item tracking_number="459323" manufacturer="Not listed">
        <item_type>Fiberglass Prehung Entry Door</item_type>
        <description>6-panel left-hand inswing entry door,
primed, white</description>
    </item>
    <item tracking_number="459789" manufacturer="Not listed">
        <item_type>Steel Prehung Entry Door</item_type>
```

```
      <description>4-panel left-hand inswing entry door,
primed, black, steel</description>
   </item>
</inventory>
```

the elements selected by the value-of select="item_type" declaration are:

```
<item_type>Fiberglass Prehung Entry Door</item_type>
<item_type>Steel Prehung Entry Door</item_type>
```

You can use relative paths that reference more than one level in the hierarchy as well. To do this, you reference the immediate child nodes that you want to work with and then separate each subsequent level of nodes below this node with a slash (/). For example, if the node tree looked like this:

```
-inventory
   -item
      -item_type
         -code
         -label
         -manufacturer
      -description
   -item
      -item_type
         -code
         -label
         -manufacturer
      -description
   -summary
```

and the current context node is an `item` node, you could reference the code, `label`, and `manufacturer` sub nodes with the following relative paths:

```
item_type/code
item_type/label
item_type/manufacturer
```

You could use these relative paths in match or select attributes of XSLT elements, such as:

```
<xsl:template match="item">
      <tr>
         <td>
           <xsl:value-of select="item/code"/>
         </td>
         <td>
           <xsl:value-of select="item/label"/>
         </td>
         <td>
           <xsl:value-of select="item/manufacturer"/>
         </td>
      </tr>
</xsl:template>
```

You can select children of the current node by following these steps:

1. Type ***child***, where child is the name of the node contained within the current context node.
2. Optionally, type **/grandchild** to specify a node set contained in the referenced child node. Repeat this step to go farther down the hierarchy.

The result should look similar to the following:

```
<xsl:value-of select="child/grandchild"/>
```

Using Absolute XPath Expressions with Elements

In addition to being able to reference nodes using relative paths, you can use absolute paths as well. An absolute location path always starts with a slash, which tells the XSLT processor to start with the root element regardless of the current context and then go on to specify the exact path to the node you want to work with. For example, if the node hierarchy for a document looked like this:

```
-inventory
   -item
      -item_type
         -code
```

```
         -label
         -manufacturer
      -description
   -item
      -item_type
         -code
         -label
         -manufacturer
      -description
   -summary
```

the corresponding absolute paths to nodes in the document are

- **/inventory/item** The absolute path to top-level item nodes
- **/inventory/item/item_type** The absolute path to item_type nodes that are child nodes of the top-level node item
- **/inventory/item/item_type/code** The absolute path to code nodes that are child nodes of the item_type node, which are in turn child nodes of the top-level node item
- **/inventory/item/item_type/label** The absolute path to label nodes that are child nodes of the item_type node, which are in turn child nodes of the top-level node item
- **/inventory/item/item_type/manufacturer** The absolute path to manufacturer nodes that are child nodes of the item_type node, which are in turn child nodes of the top-level node item
- **/inventory/item/description** The absolute path to description nodes that are child nodes of the top-level node item
- **/inventory/summary** The absolute path to top-level summary nodes

To disregard the current context and specify an absolute path to a node, follow these steps:

1. Type / to indicate that you're specifying an absolute path that starts at the root node.
2. Type ***root***, where *root* is the name of the root node.
3. Type ***/container***, where *container* is the name of the element on the next level that contains the desired node. Repeat this step as necessary until you've specified all the ancestors of the node you're looking for.
4. Type ***/element***, where *element* is the name of the element that you want to select or match.

The result should look similar to the following:

```
<xsl:value-of select="/root/container/element"/>
```

Locating Nodes

XPath locations don't have to reference element nodes. They can also reference attribute, text, comment, and processing instruction nodes. Techniques for working with these node types are discussed in the following sections.

> **Note** Don't worry, you don't have to learn a whole new syntax to locate nonelement nodes. Everything you learned about locating elements applies to attribute, text, comment, and processing instruction nodes as well.

Working with Attribute Nodes

You reference attribute nodes using the at sign (@), followed by the name of the attribute. For example, if you wanted to reference an attribute called `tracking_number`, you'd use the XPath expression:

```
@tracking_number
```

As with elements, attributes can be located using relative or absolute paths. This means you could select the current context node's `tracking_number` attribute with the following declaration:

```
<xsl:value-of select="@tracking_number"/>
```

and that you could reference the relative path to another element's attribute, such as:

```
<xsl:value-of select="item/@tracking_number"/>
```

Here, you reference the tracking number attribute of the item element that's a child of the current context node.

Following the techniques discussed earlier in the chapter, you could reference attributes of parent elements as well, such as:

```
<xsl:value-of select="../@tracking_number"/>
```

and attributes of sibling elements, such as:

```
<xsl:value-of select="../item/@tracking_number"/>
```

You could also reference the absolute path to another element's attribute, such as:

```
<xsl:value-of select="/inventory/item/@tracking_number"/>
```

Regardless of the technique you use, the result is the same. The value of the attribute is output at the current location in the output document. For example, if the current context pointed to the `item` element that contained a `tracking_number` attribute and you wanted to display its value, you'd use the following template rule to do this:

```
<xsl:template match="item">
  <p>
    <xsl:value-of select="@tracking_number"/>
  </p>
</xsl:template>
```

Of course, a rule that processes an attribute doesn't have to be the only selection in a template. You could define multiple selections as well, such as:

```
<xsl:template match="item">
  <p>
    <xsl:value-of select="@tracking_number"/>,
    <xsl:value-of select="item_type"/>,
    <xsl:value-of select="description"/>
  </p>
</xsl:template>
```

or

```
<xsl:template match="item">
```

```
  <tr>
    <td>
      <xsl:value-of select="@tracking_number"/>
    </td>
    <td>
      <xsl:value-of select="item_type"/>
    </td>
    <td>
      <xsl:value-of select="description"/>
    </td>
  </tr>
</xsl:template>
```

You could also create a separate template rule for an attribute, such as:

```
<xsl:template match="/">
    <html>
      <body>
  <xsl:apply-templates
       select="/inventory/item/item_type/@tracking_number"/>
  <xsl:apply-templates select="/inventory/item/description"/>
      </body>
    </html>
</xsl:template>

<xsl:template
match="/inventory/item/item_type/@tracking_number">
  <h1>
    <xsl:value-of select="."/>
  </h1>
</xsl:template>

<xsl:template match="/inventory/item/description">
  <p>
    <xsl:value-of select="."/>
  </p>
</xsl:template>
```

To select a node's attribute or attributes, follow these steps:

1. Specify the absolute or relative path to the attribute that you want to select or match. If the attribute is contained in the current context node, you don't need to do this.
2. Type **@*attribute***, where *attribute* is the name of the attribute you want to work with. Or type **@*** to select all attributes of the current or specified element.

The result should look similar to the following:

```
<xsl:value-of select="element/@attribute"/>
```

Working with Text Nodes

If an element contains text or CDATA sections, you can use the text() node test to select and display that text. For example, if you wanted to select the text and then do something with it, you could define a template rule like this:

```
<xsl:template match="item">
  <xsl:apply-templates select="item_type/text()"/>
</xsl:template>

<xsl:template match="item_type/text()">
  <p>
    <xsl:value-of select="."/>
  </p>
</xsl:template>
```

Or you could display the text directly using a value-of declaration like this:

```
<xsl:template match="item">
  <p>
    <xsl:value-of select="item_type/text()"/>
  </p>
</xsl:template>
```

Keep in mind that the text() node test selects all the text-node children of the context node. This means that the result is always the concatenation of all text and CDATA sections that an element contains.

To display the text associated with an element, follow these steps:

1. Specify the absolute or relative path to the element that contains the text you want to select. If the text is contained in the current context node, you don't need to do this.
2. Type **text()**.

The result should look similar to the following:

```
<xsl:value-of select="element/text()"/>
```

Working with Comment Nodes

To access comment nodes, you use the comment() node test. Working with comment nodes is similar to working with text nodes. If you wanted to access the comment node associated with an item element, you could use a relative XPath expression, such as item/comment(), or an absolute XPath expression, such as /inventory/item/comment().

A template rule that works with a comment node could look like this:

```
<xsl:template match="item">
  <xsl:apply-templates select="item_type/comment()"/>
</xsl:template>

<xsl:template match="item_type/comment()">
  <p>
    <xsl:value-of select="."/>
  </p>
</xsl:template>
```

Or you could display the comment text directly using a value-of declaration like this:

```
<xsl:template match="item">
  <p>
```

```
    <xsl:value-of select="item_type/comment()"/>
  </p>
</xsl:template>
```

The comment() node test selects all the comment-node children of the context node. This means that the result is always the concatenation of all comments that an element contains.

To display the comment text associated with an element, follow these steps:

1. Specify the absolute or relative path to the element that contains the comment text you want to select. If the comment text is contained in the current context node, you don't need to do this.
2. Type comment().

The result should look similar to the following:

```
<xsl:value-of select="element/comment()"/>
```

Working with Processing Instruction Nodes

You use the processing-instruction() node test to access processing instruction nodes. As with other node types, you can access processing instruction nodes using relative or absolute XPath locations, such as ../processing-instruction() or /inventory/item/processing-instruction().

By default, this node test selects the text of all processing-instruction-node children of the context node. As a result, results returned by the processing-instruction() node test contain the concatenation of all processing instructions that an element contains. Because processing instructions have two parts: a name and a value, you can also reference specific processing instructions by name. The format you follow is:

```
processing-instruction('name')
```

where name is the actual name of the processing instruction. For example, if you wanted to access the `xml-stylesheet` processing instruction, you'd use the value:

```
processing-instruction('xml-stylesheet')
```

Here, the XSLT processor would select all processing-instruction-node children of the context node that have the name xml-stylesheet.

To display the contents of processing instructions associated with an element, follow these steps:

1. Specify the absolute or relative path to the element that contains the processing instruction you want to select. If the processing instruction is contained in the current context node, you don't need to do this.
2. With named processing instructions, you can type **processing-instruction(*'name'*)**, where name is the name of the processing instruction that you want to select. Or you can select all processing instructions associated with the current or specified element by typing **processing-instruction()**.

The result should look similar to the following:

```
<xsl:value-of select="element/processing-
instruction('name')"/>
```

Using Namespaces with Element and Attribute Nodes

XSLT processors track namespaces using namespace nodes. Every element and attribute node defined in a document can have a namespace associated with it. Whenever a namespace is defined, you must reference the qualified name in your XSLT stylesheets. As discussed in *XML, DTDs, Schemas: The Personal Trainer*, a qualified name has two parts:

- A namespace prefix
- A local part

and follows the form:

```
namespace_prefix:local_part
```

This means that the qualified name for an `item` element in the inv namespace is `inv:item` and this element would be used in a document like this:

```
<inv:item>
...
</inv:item>
```

XPath defines three functions that allow you to work with element and attribute names. These functions are

- **name()** Returns the qualified name of an element or attribute. For the inv:item element, the function would return inv:item.
- **local-name()** Returns the local-part name of an element or attribute. For the inv:item element, the function would return item.
- **namespace-uri()** Returns the namespace prefix associated with an element or attribute. For the inv:item element, the function would return inv.

You can use these functions much as you use other XPath functions. Here's an example that uses these functions as part of a selection:

```
<xsl:template match="inv:item">
  <p>Qualified Name:
    <xsl:value-of select="name()"/>
  </p>
  <p>Local-part Name:
    <xsl:value-of select="local-name()"/>
  </p>
  <p>Namespace prefix:
    <xsl:value-of select="namespace-uri()"/>
  </p>
</xsl:template>
```

To display a node's name, follow these steps:

1. Specify the absolute or relative path to the node you want to select. You don't need to do this if you want to work with the current node context.
2. To display the qualified name of the node, type **name()**. Otherwise, type **namespace-uri()** or **local-name()** to select the part of the qualified name that you want to work with.

The result should look similar to the following:

```
<xsl:value-of select="element/name()"/>
```

Using Wildcards and Predicates in XPath Expressions

So far this chapter has discussed the primary expression operators but hasn't discussed wildcard or predicate operators. The following sections look at these XPath operators (with the exception of $, which is discussed in the next chapter).

Selecting Any Node

XPath defines three operators that can help you select multiple nodes as part of an expression. These operators are

- ***** Selects any node of the principal node type. This means that if you're working with element nodes, you can use * to select or match any element node in the current context.
- **@*** Selects any attribute node in the current context.
- **node()** Selects all nodes in the current context regardless of type.

To understand how you could use these operators, consider the following node tree representation:

```
-inventory
   -item
       @code
       @label
       @manufacturer
       -description
       -summary
   -item
       @code
       @label
       @manufacturer
       -description
       -summary
```

Here, `code`, `label`, and `manufacturer` are selected attributes of `item` and `description` and `summary` are child elements of `item`. If the `item` element is the current context node, you could create a template that selects and displays the value of `description` and `summary` child elements like this:

```
<xsl:template match="item">
  <p><xsl:value-of select="*"/></p>
</xsl:template>
```

If you wanted to select all attributes of item, you could change the template to read:

```
<xsl:template match="item">
  <p><xsl:value-of select="@*"/></p>
</xsl:template>
```

Or you could select all child elements and attributes using:

```
<xsl:template match="item">
  <p><xsl:value-of select="*|@*"/></p>
</xsl:template>
```

Here, the | pipe symbol indicates a series where either the * or the @* operator can be used in the selection. The result is that all child elements and all attributes are selected.

Still, if you wanted, you could extend the selection node set even further using node(), such as:

```
<xsl:template match="item">
  <p><xsl:value-of select="node()"/></p>
</xsl:template>
```

With the node() node test, all nodes in the current context are selected, including element, attribute, comment, and processing-instruction nodes. Of course, in an actual document you'd probably want to format the output in a more meaningful way than with simple paragraphs.

To select any node, follow these steps:

1. Specify the absolute or relative path to the nodes that you want to select or match. If the nodes are contained within the current context, you don't need to do this.
2. Specify the type of nodes to select or match:

- Type * to match nodes of the current type. Typically, this match is for element nodes.
- Type **@*** to select all attribute nodes of the current or specified element.
- Type **node()** to select all nodes of any type associated with the current or specified node.

The result should look similar to the following:

```
<xsl:value-of select="element/*"/>
```

Skipping Levels in the Hierarchy

The double slash operator (//) allows you to skip levels in the node tree hierarchy. This indicator tells the XSLT processor that zero or more elements may occur between the slashes and lets the XSLT processor search down the hierarchy for the node you're referencing.

To see how the double slash operator (//) works, consider the following node tree representation:

```
-inventory
   -item
      -item_type
        -description
           -code
           -label
           -manufacturer
        -summary
   -item
      -item_type
        -description
           -code
           -label
           -manufacturer
        -summary
```

Here the absolute paths to the lowest-level elements (`code`, `label`, and `manufacturer`) are

- /inventory/item/item_type/description/code
- /inventory/item/item_type/description/label
- /inventory/item/item_type/description/manufacturer

If you wanted to skip levels in the hierarchy using //, you could do this in several ways. Here are some examples:

- **//code** Starts from the root element and selects all code elements regardless of where they appear in the document
- **/inventory//code** Selects all code elements that are descendants of the inventory element
- **/inventory/item//code** Selects all code elements that are descendants of the top-level item element
- **//description/code** Selects all code elements that have the parent element description
- **.//code** Selects all code elements that are descendants of the current context node

> **Caution** Although being able to skip levels in the hierarchy is very powerful, watch out! Skipping through the hierarchy requires the XSLT processor to search through the node tree for successive matches, which can be very inefficient in large documents with lots of nodes.

To select skip levels in the hierarchy, follow these steps:

1. As necessary, specify the absolute or relative path to the nodes that you want to select or match. When you get to the levels that you want to skip, type //.
2. As necessary, type the path to the nodes that you want to work with.
3. Type the name of the element node you want to select or match. Alternatively, type @ followed by the name of the attribute node you want to select or match.

The result should look similar to the following:

```
<xsl:value-of select=".//element/@attribute"/>
```

Filtering To Match Nodes

You use the [] operator to specify a predicate. Predicate expressions are used to filter a group of nodes according to their position in a node set or according to a specific match value. XSLT processors evaluate predication expressions as Boolean values, which are either true or false. If a predicate expression is true, the node is a match and is selected. Otherwise, the node isn't selected.

Predicate expressions have the basic form:

```
path[predicate]
```

where *path* is the location path to the node that contains the desired subset of nodes you want to work with and *predicate* is the predicate expression that defines your filter for this set of nodes.

If you're referencing nodes in the current context, the predicate can be used without a path. In the following example the predicate expression returns all nodes that have a tracking_number attribute:

```
<xsl:apply-templates select="[@tracking_number]"/>
```

Numeric positions, functions, and attribute values can be referenced in predicate expressions as well. For example, the following predication expression selects the second item element in the current context:

```
<xsl:apply-templates select="item[2]"/>
```

If the input document contains at least two `item` elements, the node set for the second `item` is returned. Otherwise, an empty node set is returned.

Using Numeric Positions in Predicates

When the current context points to a set of nodes, each node can be referred to by its position in the node set. The first element has the position 1, the second has the position 2, and so on. You can refer to the numeric position directly in the predicate expression and you can combine numeric references with other operators and expressions. For example, if you wanted to select the fifth `item` element, you could use:

```
<xsl:apply-templates select="item[5]"/>
```

In an XPath expression, the choice operator (|) selects either match in a series. Because nodes are processed recursively and node sets can contain multiple nodes, a value of match="a|b|c" says to match elements named a, b, or c. You could match numeric values in the same way. For example, if you wanted to select the second, fourth, and sixth `item` elements, you could combine the choice operator (|) with numeric positions, such as:

```
<xsl:apply-templates select="item[2|4|6]"/>
```

or you could use:

```
<xsl:apply-templates select="item[2] | item[4] | item[6]"/>
```

Using Functions in Predicates

You can also use XPath functions with predicate expressions. The most common functions you'll use are

- **last()** Returns the last node in the context subset.
- **position()** Returns the current position within the context subset. You can use this in expressions to evaluate the current position within a subset with a desired position.

Returning the last node in a set is easy. For example, if you wanted to select the last `item` element in a node set, you'd specify:

```
<xsl:apply-templates select="item[last()]"/>
```

When you combine the position() function with arithmetic operators, you can use the resulting expressions to obtain just about any node in the context subset that you want to work with. For example, if you wanted to select the third `item` node in the node set, you'd specify:

```
<xsl:apply-templates select="item[position() = 3]"/>
```

Here the equals sign is a Boolean operator. If the position of the `item` element is 3, the expression is true and the matching node is selected. Otherwise, the expression is false and a node isn't selected.

The less than (<), greater than (>), less than or equals (<=), and greater than or equals (>=) operators are useful in expressions. For example, if you wanted to select nodes 1-5 in the node set, you could specify:

```
<xsl:apply-templates select="[position() <= 5]"/>
```

Another useful operator is mod. The mod operator returns the remainder after division. If you note that any value mod 2 either returns a 0 or a value greater than 0, you can use mod to select even-numbered or odd-numbered nodes. For example, if you wanted to return only even-numbered item elements, you'd specify:

```
<xsl:apply-templates select="item[position() mod 2 = 0]"/>
```

For only odd-numbered item elements, you'd specify:

```
<xsl:apply-templates select="item[position() mod 2 != 0]"/>
```

Using Attribute Values in Predicates

You can also use predicate expressions to select attributes by name or by value. To see how expressions that use attributes work, consider the following XML document:

```
<?xml version="1.0" ?>
<inventory>
   <item tracking_number="459320" manufacturer="MHWB
Industries">
      <item_type>Fiberglass Prehung Entry Door</item_type>
      <description>6-panel left-hand inswing entry door,
primed, white</description>
      <stock in_stock="750" orders_for="200" net_units="550"
order="N" />
   </item>
   <item tracking_number="459323" manufacturer="Not listed">
      <item_type>Fiberglass Prehung Entry Door</item_type>
```

```
        <description>6-panel left-hand inswing entry door,
primed, white</description>
        <stock in_stock="50" orders_for="200" net_units="-150"
order="Y" />
    </item>
    <item tracking_number="459780" manufacturer="MHWB
Industries">
        <item_type>Steel Prehung Entry Door</item_type>
        <description>4-panel left-hand inswing entry door,
primed, black, steel</description>
        <stock in_stock="250" orders_for="200" net_units="50"
order="Y" />
    </item>
    <item tracking_number="459789" manufacturer="Not listed">
        <item_type>Steel Prehung Entry Door</item_type>
        <description>4-panel left-hand inswing entry door,
primed, black, steel</description>
        <stock in_stock="0" orders_for="200" net_units="-200"
order="Y" />
    </item>

...
</inventory>
```

Using this document as our input, we could work with the document's attribute nodes in several ways. If you wanted to select all `item` elements with `tracking_number` attributes, you could specify:

```
<xsl:apply-templates select="item[@tracking_number]"/>
```

If you wanted to select `item` elements with specific tracking numbers, you simply specify values that represent a match. In this example items with tracking numbers 459780 and 459789 are selected:

```
<xsl:apply-templates select="item[@tracking_number='459780'|
@tracking_number='459789']"/>
```

Note It's important to Note that in this example double quotation marks are used to contain the entire selection and single quotation marks are used for attribute values. You could have also used single quotation marks to contain the selection and double quotation marks for attribute values. However, you couldn't use the same type of quotation marks to contain the selection and designate the attribute values. Further, you can't start a selection with double quotation marks and end it with single quotation marks.

Now imagine that this document contained hundreds of items but the user viewing the document only cared about certain items: those that didn't list a manufacturer (representing an entry error) and those that that had an order flag value of "Y" (indicating items that needed to be ordered to meet current demand). If this were the case, you could create predicate expressions that matched these values:

- item_type/[@manufacturer='Not listed']
- item_type/[@order='Y']

Then use the expressions in select and match statements to obtain the desired results. The following XSLT stylesheet shows a partial example:

```
<xsl:template match="/">
    <html>
      <body>
  <xsl:apply-templates select="inventory/item"/>
      </body>
    </html>
</xsl:template>

<xsl:template match="item">
  <xsl:apply-templates select="item_type/[@manufacturer='Not
listed']"/>
  <xsl:apply-templates select="item_type/[@order='Y']"/>
</xsl:template>
```

```
<xsl:template match="item_type/[@manufacturer='Not listed']">
...
</xsl:template>

<xsl:template match="item_type/[@order='Y']">
...
</xsl:template>
```

Specifying the Node Subset in a Stylesheet

Now that you've seen how predicates are used, you can use predicates in your XSLT stylesheets anywhere you want to filter a group of nodes and specify a node subset.

To select any node, follow these steps:

1. Specify the absolute or relative path to the node that contains the desired subset of nodes. If you want to work with a subset of nodes in the current context, you don't have to specify a path.
2. Type [***expression***], where *expression* represents the predicate expression that you want to use to select the node subset.

The result should look similar to the following:

```
<xsl:value-of select="element/[expression]"/>
```

Chapter 3. Branching & Control Functions

As with any sophisticated programming language, the XSL Transformations (XSLT) language defines structures that you can use to add branching and control logic to stylesheets. You use branching and control functions to conditionally process nodes based on the value of an expression. XSLT implements most of the classic branching and control functions, including

- **if-then** With if-then, you can specify what processing should occur if a value matches an expression. In XSLT, if-then structures are implemented using the `xsl:if` element.
- **if-then-else** With if-then-else, you can specify what processing should occur when a value matches an expression and when a value doesn't match an expression. In XSLT, if-then-else structures are implemented using the `xsl:choose` and `xsl:otherwise` elements.
- **switch-case** With switch-case, you can specify a set of values that should be matched and what should happen in the case of each match. You can also specify what happens when no match is found. In XSLT switch-case structures are implemented using the `xsl:choose` and `xsl:when` elements, and the case for no match is handled with the `xsl:otherwise` element.
- **for-each** With for-each, you can specify what processing should occur for each value in a set of values. In XSLT this concept allows you to process all nodes in a set of nodes iteratively and the element you use to do this is the `xsl:for-each` element.

In this chapter you'll learn how to use these branching and control functions. You'll also learn how to control which templates are called, included, or imported.

Processing with if Statements

With if statements, you can specify what processing should occur if a value matches an expression. The XSLT structure that you use to define an if statement is the `xsl:if` element. This element has a single attribute, called `test`, that's used to specify the expression that you want to match. If `test` evaluates to the Boolean value true, the statements between the opening tag <xsl:if> and the closing tag </xsl:if> are processed.

The basic format of an if statement is then:

```
<xsl:if test="expression">
...
</xsl:if>
```

where *expression* is an XML Path (XPath) expression defining what you want to test. Following this basic format, you could define an if statement to test the value of an expression, like this:

```
<xsl:if test="stock/[@order='Y']">
 <p>Please order, stock number: <xsl:value-of
select="@tracking_number"/>
 </p>
</xsl:if>
```

Here, you define an expression that checks the `order` attribute of the `stock` element, which is a child of the current context node. If the value of the attribute is Y, the value of the `tracking_number` attribute of the node being processed is output as part of an HTML paragraph, such as:

```
<p>Please order, stock number: 459323</p>
```

The if statement could appear anywhere within the template you're defining. Here's an example:

```
<xsl:template match="/">
    <html>
      <body>
        <xsl:apply-templates select="inventory/item"/>
      </body>
    </html>
</xsl:template>

<xsl:template match="item">
  <xsl:if test="stock/[@order='Y']">
   <p>Please order, stock number: <xsl:value-of
select="@tracking_number"/>
   </p>
  </xsl:if>
```

```
</xsl:template>
```

> **Tip** The most important thing to keep in mind when working with `xsl:if` is that every expression evaluates to a Boolean value that's either true or false—there's no exception.

You'll find that if statements are useful when you want to perform basic value tests, such as determining whether a value is a number or a string. Here's a brief summary that details how datatypes are converted to Boolean values:

- **node-set** If a node-set contains one or more nodes, the node-set test evaluates to true. Otherwise, the node-set test evaluates to false. Examples follow:

  <xsl:if test="item/item_type"> If the current context contains one or more `item` elements that in turn contain one or more `item_type` elements, this test evaluates to true. Otherwise, the test is false.

  <xsl:if test=".//@tracking_number"> If the current context contains one or more descendants that have a `tracking_number` attribute, this test evaluates to true. Otherwise, the test is false.

- **number** If a number is greater than or less than zero, the number test evaluates to true. If the number is positive zero, negative zero, or NaN, the number test evaluates to false.

  <xsl:if test="count(item/item_type) >= 5"> If the current context contains one or more `item` elements that in turn contain five or more `item_type` elements, this test evaluates to true. Otherwise, the test is false.

> **Real World** When you use <, <=, >, or >= as part of an attribute value, you should escape the < or > sign to ensure that the XSLT processor interprets the operator correctly. This means you should enter < for <, <= for <=, > for >, and >= for >=.

<xsl:if test="number(@total_sales)"> If the current context element has an attribute called `total_sales` that's a valid number, this test evaluates to true. Otherwise, the test is false. For example, if the attribute has string value, such as "Hello", the test would evaluate to false.

- **string** If a string contains one or more characters, the string test evaluates to true. Otherwise, the string test evaluates to false.

  <xsl:if test="string(@manufacturer)"> If the current context element has an attribute called `manufacturer` that's a valid string, this test evaluates to true. Otherwise, the test is false.

  <xsl:if test="$x"> If the variable contains a value that meets the criteria for its respective datatype (either string, number or node-set), this test evaluates to true. Otherwise, the test is false. For example, if the variable represented a number and contained the value 0, the test would evaluate to false. However, if the variable represented a number and contained the value 25, the test would evaluate to true.

You can implement if statements in XSLT stylesheets by completing the following steps:

1. Within a template rule, type **<xsl:if test="*expression*">**, where *expression* is an XPath expression defining what you want to test.
2. Specify what should happen if the expression evaluates to true.
3. Type </xsl:if>.

Processing with choose Statements

XSLT defines elements that you can use to specify a set of values that should be matched and what should happen in the case of a match. You can also specify what happens when no match is found. These elements are:

- **xsl:choose** The `xsl:choose` element is used to enclose a set of choices. The opening tag <xsl:choose> marks the beginning of the choices that you want to match and the closing tag </xsl:choose> marks the ending of those choices.
- **xsl:when** The `xsl:when` element is used to specify the test expression that you want to match and to enclose the set of statements that should be processed in case of a match. An `xsl:when` element has the same syntax as an `xsl:if` element, complete with a test attribute.

- **xsl:otherwise** The `xsl:otherwise` element is used to specify what should happen when no match is found in the list of when choices.

The basic format of a choose-when structure is:

```
<xsl:choose>
  <xsl:when test="expression1">
  ...
  </xsl:when>
  <xsl:when test="expression2">
  ...
  </xsl:when>
  <xsl:when test="expressionN">
  ...
  </xsl:when>
</xsl:choose>
```

where *expression1*, *expression2*, ..., *expressionN* are the expressions you want to test. Only the statements associated with the first match found are processed.

You can extend choose-when to include a default choice that's used when no match is found. You implement the default choice using the `xsl:otherwise` element. The basic format of a choose-when-otherwise structure is:

```
<xsl:choose>
  <xsl:when test="expression1">
  ...
  </xsl:when>
  <xsl:when test="expression2">
  ...
  </xsl:when>
  <xsl:when test="expressionN">
  ...
  </xsl:when>
  <xsl:otherwise>
  ...
  </xsl:otherwise >
```

```
</xsl:choose>
```

To see how choices use expressions, consider the following example:

```
<xsl:template match="/">
    <html>
      <body>
        <xsl:apply-templates select="inventory/item"/>
      </body>
    </html>
</xsl:template>

<xsl:template match="item">
  <xsl:choose>
    <xsl:when test=" stock/[@order='Y']">
      <p>Please order, stock number:
      <xsl:value-of select="@tracking_number"/>
     </p>
    </xsl:when>
    <xsl:when test=" stock/[@order='N']">
      <p>Item <xsl:value-of select="@tracking_number"/>
      doesn't need to be re-stocked at this time.</p>
    </xsl:when>
    <xsl:otherwise>
      <p>INVALID ORDER INDICATOR FOR ITEM:
      <xsl:value-of select="@tracking_number"/>
      </p>
    </xsl:otherwise>
  </xsl:choose>
</xsl:template>
```

In this example you define expressions that check the `order` attribute of the `stock` element, which is a child of the current context node. If the value of the `order` attribute is Y, the first when statement is a match for the expression and, as a result, the output specifies that the item should be ordered. If the value of the `order` attribute is N, the second when statement is a match for the expression, and, as a result, the output specifies that the item doesn't need to be ordered. On the other hand, if the `order` attribute doesn't contain a Y or N, an error indicator is output.

You can use choose-when and choose-when-otherwise in XSLT stylesheets by completing the following steps:

1. Within a template rule, type **<xsl:choose>** to mark the beginning of the choice set.
2. Type **<xsl:when test="*expression*">**, where *expression* is an XPath expression defining what you want to test.
3. Specify what should happen if the expression evaluates to true.
4. Type </xsl:when>.
5. Repeat steps 2-4 for each condition.
6. If you want to specify an option to be used if no match is found, type **<xsl:otherwise>**, specify what should happen if none of the previously specified conditions are true, and then type **</xsl:otherwise>**.
7. Type **</xsl:choose>** to complete the choice set.

Caution The first match (and only the first match) is used. All other conditions that follow a match are ignored. This differs from switch-case implementations in most programming languages where a break statement is required to drop out of the switch-case construct.

Processing with for-each Statements

If you want to process all nodes that match a certain criteria, you can use the `xsl:for-each` element. This element lets you specify a set of nodes with a select attribute and then perform iterative processing on each node in the node set.

The basic format of a for-each statement is:

```
<xsl:for-each select="expression">
...
```

```
</xsl:for-each>
```

where *expression* is an XPath expression that returns a node set.

To see how for-each statements work, consider the following input document:

```
<?xml version="1.0" ?>
<inventory>
   <item tracking_number="459320" manufacturer="MHWB
Industries">
      <item_type>Fiberglass Prehung Entry Door</item_type>
      <description>6-panel left-hand inswing entry door,
primed, white</description>
      <stock in_stock="750" orders_for="200" net_units="550"
order="N" />
   </item>
   <item tracking_number="459323" manufacturer="Not listed">
      <item_type>Fiberglass Prehung Entry Door</item_type>
      <description>6-panel left-hand inswing entry door,
primed, white</description>
      <stock in_stock="50" orders_for="200" net_units="-150"
order="Y" />
   </item>
   <item tracking_number="459780" manufacturer="MHWB
Industries">
      <item_type>Steel Prehung Entry Door</item_type>
      <description>4-panel left-hand inswing entry door,
primed, black, steel</description>
      <stock in_stock="250" orders_for="200" net_units="50"
order="Y" />
   </item>
   <item tracking_number="459789" manufacturer="Not listed">
      <item_type>Steel Prehung Entry Door</item_type>
      <description>4-panel left-hand inswing entry door,
primed, black, steel</description>
      <stock in_stock="0" orders_for="200" net_units="-200"
order="Y" />
   </item>
</inventory>
```

This document contains a list of inventory items. Although there are currently only four items in the document, you can imagine a case where there are dozens, hundreds, or thousands of items that you want to process in some way. You could define a stylesheet that processes these elements in the traditional recursive manner, such as:

```
<xsl:template match="/">
    <html>
      <body>
  <xsl:apply-templates select="inventory/item"/>
      </body>
    </html>
</xsl:template>

<xsl:template match="item">
  <xsl:apply-templates select="item_type"/>
  <xsl:apply-templates select="description"/>
  <xsl:apply-templates select="stock"/>
</xsl:template>

<xsl:template match="item_type">
...
</xsl:template>

<xsl:template match="description">
...
</xsl:template>

<xsl:template match="stock">
...
</xsl:template>
```

However, the structure of the inventory document is such that you could also iteratively process the document at the `item` element level to obtain all the necessary information. You might prefer iterative processing if you simply want to extract and display the values associated with the child elements: `item_type`, `description`, and `stock`.

One way to iteratively process the inventory document using for-each statements follows:

```
<xsl:template match="/">
    <html>
      <body>
        <table>
            <tr>
                <th>Inv Number</th>
                <th>Item</th>
                <th>Manufacturer</th>
                <th>Current</th>
                <th>Orders</th>
                <th>Remaining</th>
            </tr>
            <xsl:for-each select="inventory/item">
            <tr>
                <td><xsl:value-of
select="@tracking_number"/></td>
                <td><xsl:value-of select="item_type"/></td>
                <td><xsl:value-of
select="@manufacturer"/></td>
                <td><xsl:value-of
select="stock/@in_stock"/></td>
                <td><xsl:value-of
select="stock/@orders_for"/></td>
                <td><xsl:value-of
select="stock/@net_units"/></td>
              </tr>
            </xsl:for-each>
        </table>
      </body>
    </html>
</xsl:template>
```

In this example the root node is the context node that you're working with. Each time the XSLT processor encounters a child node of the root node that's an `item` element, the select expression in the for-each statement is matched. The body of the for-each statement builds a table row that contains values that you want to output. The result is the following HTML document:

```
<html>
  <body>
    <table>
      <tr>
        <th>Inv Number</th>
        <th>Item</th>
        <th>Manufacturer</th>
        <th>Current</th>
        <th>Orders</th>
        <th>Remaining</th>
      </tr>
      <tr>
         <td>459320</td>
         <td>Fiberglass Prehung Entry Door</td>
         <td>MHWB Industries</td>
         <td>750</td>
         <td>200</td>
         <td>550</td>
       </tr>
      <tr>
         <td>459323</td>
         <td>Fiberglass Prehung Entry Door</td>
         <td>Not listed</td>
         <td>50</td>
         <td>200</td>
         <td>-150</td>
       </tr>
      <tr>
         <td>459780</td>
         <td>Steel Prehung Entry Door</td>
         <td>MHWB Industries</td>
         <td>250</td>
         <td>200</td>
         <td>50</td>
       </tr>
      <tr>
         <td>459789</td>
```

```
            <td>Steel Prehung Entry Door</td>
            <td>Not listed</td>
            <td>0</td>
            <td>200</td>
            <td>-200</td>
        </tr>
    </table>
  </body>
</html>
```

You can use for-each statements in XSLT stylesheets by completing the following steps:

1. Within a template rule, type **<xsl:for-each select="*expression*">**, where *expression* is an XPath expression that returns a node set.
2. Specify what should happen, the processing that should occur, for each matching node.
3. Type </xsl:for-each>.

Invoking, Including, and Importing Templates

So far we've always assumed that the template rules you want to work with are in the current stylesheet and that you want to recursively or iteratively process template rules. While this is true in most cases, sometimes you'll want to

- Call templates directly by name
- Include or import templates from one stylesheet in another stylesheet
- Define multiple template rules that can be applied to the same set of nodes

Techniques for performing these tasks are examined in the sections that follow.

Including and Importing Templates

When you want to work with templates defined in other stylesheets, you can include or import the stylesheets containing those templates. The elements you use to include or import stylesheets are `xsl:include` and `xsl:import`, respectively.

Defining Include Statements

You define an include statement like this:

```
<xsl:include href="URLpath/filename" />
```

where *URLpath/filename* is the actual URL and filename of the stylesheet you want to include, such as:

```
<xsl:include href="../mystyles.xsl" />
```

With an include statement, you can insert the template rules defined in another stylesheet anywhere in the contents of the current stylesheet. Because the template rules in the included stylesheet have the same priority as template rules in the original stylesheet, any conflicts are resolved according to the order in which the template rules are entered in the merged stylesheet (essentially, the XSLT processor uses the first template rule with a name that matches the select value of the apply-templates declaration).

In most cases you'll use included stylesheets when you want to define template rules containing standard markup elements, such as those for the header and footer of an HTML document. To see how this would work, consider the following example:

```
<xsl:stylesheet version="2.0"
  xmlns:xsl="http://www.w3.org/1999/XSL/Transform">

  <xsl:output method="html"/>

<xsl:template match="/">
    <html>
      <body>
  <xsl:apply-templates
       select="/inventory/item/item_type/@tracking_number"/>
  <xsl:apply-templates select="/inventory/item/description"/>
      </body>
    </html>
</xsl:template>
```

```
  <xsl:include href="inventory.xsl" />

</xsl:stylesheet>
```

Here you have the definition of the original stylesheet that has an include statement for a stylesheet named inventory.xsl. If the contents of the inventory.xsl stylesheet are:

```
<xsl:stylesheet version="2.0"
  xmlns:xsl="http://www.w3.org/1999/XSL/Transform">

<xsl:template
match="/inventory/item/item_type/@tracking_number">
  <h1>
    <xsl:value-of select="."/>
  </h1>
</xsl:template>

<xsl:template match="/inventory/item/description">
  <p>
    <xsl:value-of select="."/>
  </p>
</xsl:template>

</xsl:stylesheet>
```

the result of the include is a stylesheet that XSLT processors interpret as:

```
<xsl:stylesheet version="2.0"
  xmlns:xsl="http://www.w3.org/1999/XSL/Transform">

  <xsl:output method="html"/>

<xsl:template match="/">
    <html>
      <body>
  <xsl:apply-templates
       select="/inventory/item/item_type/@tracking_number"/>
  <xsl:apply-templates select="/inventory/item/description"/>
```

```
      </body>
    </html>
</xsl:template>

<xsl:template
match="/inventory/item/item_type/@tracking_number">
  <h1>
    <xsl:value-of select="."/>
  </h1>
</xsl:template>

<xsl:template match="/inventory/item/description">
  <p>
    <xsl:value-of select="."/>
  </p>
</xsl:template>

</xsl:stylesheet>
```

You can include a stylesheet in another stylesheet by completing these steps:

1. Compare the stylesheet(s) that you want to include in another stylesheet, looking for possible conflicts where template rules have the same match expression. If you find possible conflicts, be sure to pay particular attention to the location in which you insert the stylesheet.
2. At the point in the original stylesheet where you want to include another stylesheet, type **<xsl:include href="URIpath/filename" />**, where *URLpath/filename* is the actual URL and filename of the stylesheet you want to include.
3. Repeat steps 1 and 2 for other stylesheets that you want to include.

Defining Import Statements

You define an import statement like this:

```
<xsl:import href="URLpath/filename" />
```

where *URLpath/filename* is the actual URL and filename of the stylesheet you want to import, such as:

```
<xsl:import href="../mystyles.xsl" />
```

Unlike include statements, import statements must appear at the beginning of a stylesheet, immediately following the `xsl:stylesheet` element. Additionally, the imported template rules have a lower priority than rules in the current stylesheet. This means that rules in the current stylesheet always have precedence over rules in an imported stylesheet.

You can import a stylesheet into another stylesheet by completing these steps:

1. Locate the opening stylesheet tag in the original stylesheet. This tag follows the form <xsl:stylesheet>.
2. After the opening stylesheet tag, type **<xsl:import href="*URIpath/filename*" />**, where *URLpath/filename* is the actual URL and filename of the stylesheet you want to import.
3. If you want to import additional stylesheets, enter each new import declaration after the existing import declaration(s).

Calling Templates by Name

Although recursive and iterative processing are great, sometimes you want to directly access a template no matter where you are in the stylesheet and irrespective of the current context. Don't worry, XSLT does allow you to directly access a template in the current stylesheet. To do this, you call a template by name using an `xsl:call-template` element.

Calling a template is a two-part process. First, you must define a named template. The basic format for a named template is:

```
<xsl:template name="template_name">
...
</xsl:template>
```

where *template_name* is the name you'll use to call the template.

Second, you must invoke the named template using the `xsl:call-template` element. This element has the basic form:

```
<xsl:call-template name="template_name" />
```

where *template_name* is the name of the template you want to invoke.

You'll find that template calls are handy when you define standard markup components that you want to reference regularly. For example, you could define document headers and footers using named templates and then include the stylesheet that contains these templates in other stylesheets. Afterward, you could call the templates by name to invoke them as appropriate.

To summarize, to create and then call a named template, complete the following steps:

1. Type **<xsl:template name="*template_name*">**, where *template_name* is the actual name you'll use to call the template.
2. Specify the processing that should occur when the template is called.
3. Type </xsl:template>.
4. In the location from which you want to call the named template, type **<xsl:call-template name="*template_name*" />**, where *template_name* is the name you previously specified for the template.

Invoking Templates by Mode

When you define multiple template rules that match individual nodes within a node set, you might want to set a mode attribute for template rules that you select. The mode attribute allows you to define different templates that work with the same elements, yet in different ways. For example, you could define a template rule with mode="summary" and another with mode="detailed". In the first template, you could create a summary or digest of the currently selected nodes. In the second template, you could create a detailed output for the same set of nodes.

When you work with modes, you assign the mode attribute in the `xsl:apply-templates` element as well as in the `xsl:template` element. Here's an example:

```
<xsl:stylesheet version="2.0"
  xmlns:xsl="http://www.w3.org/1999/XSL/Transform">

  <xsl:output method="html"/>

<xsl:template match="/">
```

```
    <html>
      <body>
  <xsl:apply-templates select="inventory/item"
mode="summary"/>
  <xsl:apply-templates select="inventory/item"
mode="detailed"/>
      </body>
    </html>
</xsl:template>

<xsl:template match="item" mode="summary">
...
</xsl:template>

<xsl:template match="item" mode="detailed">
...
</xsl:template>

</xsl:stylesheet>
```

In this example you specify that templates should be applied using two modes: summary and detailed. You then define two sets of template rules: one for outputting the summary and another for outputting the details. Keep in mind that the actual value of the mode attribute is an arbitrary XML name. The XSLT processor only cares that the mode attribute is set; it doesn't attempt to discern what the mode designator means. Because of this, you can set the mode designator to a value that makes sense to you and to others viewing the stylesheet. For example, if you've designed a stylesheet with multiple modes and the output in the details section doesn't look right, you can quickly track the problem to the template rule defined with mode="detailed".

To specify a mode and then define a template rule that uses the mode, complete the following steps:

1. Define the template rule that uses a mode attribute by typing **<xsl:template match="*pattern*" mode="*currMode*">**, where *pattern* identifies the sections of the document to which the template should be applied and *currMode* identifies the current mode for this template rule.

2. Specify the processing that should occur when the template is called and then type **</xsl:template>** to complete the template rule.
3. In the location where you want to call this template rule, type **<xsl:apply-templates select="*expression*" mode="*currMode*" />**, where expression identifies the nodes whose template rules should be applied and matches the previously defined pattern and currMode identifies the current mode and matches the previously defined mode.

Chapter 4. Variables & Parameters in XSLT

In order to perform many advanced tasks, you'll need to be able to pass values into templates that are being processed or hold values temporarily during processing. As in a programming language, such as Java, you use parameters and variables to perform these tasks in XSL Transformations (XSLT). As you'll learn in this chapter, parameters and variables can have either a local scope or a global scope. Unlike global parameters and variables, which can be referenced anywhere in an XSLT stylesheet once they're defined, local parameters and variables have a very specific scope and can only be used in a part of the stylesheet.

Working with Parameters

XSLT defines two elements that you can use to pass parameters to a template: `xsl:param` and `xsl:with-param`. You define parameters using `xsl:param`, and you pass parameter values to templates using `xsl:with-param`.

Defining and Referencing Parameters

You define a parameter in a template using the `xsl:param` element. The `xsl:param` element has two attributes:

- **name** A required attribute that sets the name of the parameter
- **select** An optional attribute that sets the parameter to a specific value

One of the most basic ways to use a parameter is to define its values in a named template and then perform some processing based on the parameter values that you're using. Here's an example of a template that defines two parameters:

```
<xsl:template name="CircleArea">
   <xsl:param name="circumference"/>
   <xsl:param name="diameter"/>
   <xsl:value-of select="$circumference * $diameter"/>
</xsl:template>
```

Note You can define parameters in standard templates with match expressions as well. Regardless of whether you use a named or unnamed template, you must specify any parameters the template will use immediately after the opening <xsl:template> tag.

This template defines two parameters, circumference and diameter, and outputs their product. As a result, when you call this function and pass in a circumference and diameter, the output generated is the area of the circle represented by those two values.

In the previous example, note the syntax used to reference the parameters in the value-of element. You must use this syntax to reference parameters after you define them. This means that a parameter reference has the form:

$parameter_name

where *parameter_name* is the name of the parameter you've defined and want to use. As long as you reference the parameter as part of an XSLT element's attribute or text, you can use this basic syntax. However, if you want to reference parameters in attributes that you want to generate as part of the output markup, you must enclose the parameter reference in curly braces, such as:

```
{$parameter_name}
```

The curly braces tell the XSLT processor to replace the referenced value with its actual value. To see how this type of reference is made, consider the following template:

```
<xsl:template name="setTableStyle">
   <xsl:param name="border_size"/>
   <xsl:param name="width"/>
   <xsl:param name="bg_color"/>
   <table border="{$border_size}" width="{$width}"
bgcolor="{$bg_color}">
</xsl:template>
```

Here, you define a named template called setTableStyle that has three parameters:

- **border_size** Used to set the size of the table's border
- **width** Used to set the width of the table
- **bg_color** Used to set the background color for the table

After defining these parameters, you reference the parameters as part of the output markup.

> **Note** Technically, the second style of referencing parameters is called an *attribute value template*. However, it's much easier to think of this simply as a type of parameter reference.

To define a parameter without a default value, do the following:

- Within the template that you want to define the parameter, type **<xsl:param name="*parameter_name*"/>**, where *parameter_name* is the name you want to use for the parameter.

To reference a parameter, follow these steps:

1. If the parameter is used as part of the XSLT markup, type **$*parameter_name***, where *parameter_name* is the name of the parameter you previously defined and want to use.
2. If the parameter is used as part of the attribute in the output, type **{$*parameter_name*}**, where *parameter_name* is the name of the parameter you previously defined and want to use.

Setting Default Values for Parameters

If you like, you can define a default value for parameters. One way to do this is to assign the default value in the select attribute when you define the parameter. For example, you could set default values for the setTableStyle template's parameters like this:

```
<xsl:template name="setTableStyle">
   <xsl:param name="border_size" select="2"/>
   <xsl:param name="width" select="800"/>
   <xsl:param name="bg_color" select="'white'"/>
   <table border="{$border_size}" width="{$width}"
bgcolor="{$bg_color}">
</xsl:template>
```

The default values for the border_size, width, and bg_color parameters are 2, 800, and 'white', respectively. Now, if you invoke setTableStyle without setting values for these parameters, the default values are used and the output looks like this:

```
<table border="2" width="800" bgcolor="white">
```

Real World In the example, note that single quotation marks enclose the literal string value. Anytime you want to output a literal string as part of an attribute value, you must enclose the value in quotation marks. If you don't, the XSLT processor assumes you're referencing an element name. Here, the XSLT processor would have selected all white elements in the current context, which isn't what you wanted to do. If no white elements were in the current context, the output value would have been set to an empty string.

Another way to set the default value for a parameter is to include content within the `xsl:param` element. Here's an example:

```
<xsl:template name="setTableStyle">
   <xsl:param name="width">
     <xsl:value-of select="$widthA + $widthB + $widthC + 20">
   </xsl:param>

   <xsl:param name="border_size">
     <xsl:choose>
       <xsl:when test="$width &gt; 800">
         <xsl:text>5</xsl:text>
```

```
      </xsl:when>
      <xsl:when test="$width &lt;= 800">
        <xsl:text>2</xsl:text>
      </xsl:when>
    </xsl:choose>
  </xsl:param>

  <xsl:param name="bg_color">
    <xsl:text>white<xsl:text>
  </xsl:param>

  <table border="{$border_size}" width="{$width}"
bgcolor="{$bg_color}">

</xsl:template>
```

In this example you define the width parameter based on the value of other parameters plus a base value. Then you use the width value to determine the border_size that you want to set for the table. Finally, you set the bg_color to the literal text value white. As an example, widthA, widthB, and widthC could represent column widths of 200, 250, and 230 respectively, in which case the width parameter is set to 700 (200+250+230+20). Based on this value, the second when test is the one that's processed and the border_size is set to 2. Thus, the output in this case is:

```
<table border="2" width="700" bgcolor="white">
```

To define a parameter with a simple default value, follow these steps:

1. Within the template that you want to define the parameter, type **<xsl:param name="*parameter_name*"**, where *parameter_name* is the name you want to use for the parameter.
2. If you want to set a default value for the parameter, type **select="*parameter_value*"/>**, where parameter_value is the default value you want to assign to the parameter. Otherwise, type **/>**.

To define a parameter with default contents, follow these steps:

1. Within the template that you want to define the parameter, type **<xsl:param**

name="*parameter_name*">, where *parameter_name* is the name you want to use for the parameter.

2. Insert the contents of the parameter.
3. Type **</xsl:parameter>** to complete the parameter declaration.

Passing Parameter Values to Templates

You can pass parameter values to templates as part of an `xsl:call-template` or `xsl:apply-templates` selection. To do this, you use the `xsl:with-param` element and set the value of this element's select attribute to the value you want to pass to the template you're calling or applying.

The basic format of the with-param element is

```
<xsl:with-param name="parameter_name" select="parameter_value"
/>
```

where *parameter_name* is the name of the parameter you previously defined and *parameter_value* is the value you want to pass to this parameter. Because the select attribute is optional, you don't have to use it. However, if you don't pass in a value and a default value isn't defined, the XSLT processor uses an empty string ("") as the default value.

To see how parameter passing works, consider the following example:

```
<xsl:template name="SquareOrRectangleArea">
   <xsl:param name="width"/>
   <xsl:param name="height"/>
   <xsl:value-of select="$width * $height"/>
</xsl:template>
```

Here, you've defined a template that computes the area of a square or rectangle based on the value of width and height parameters. If you wanted to invoke this named template, you'd use the `xsl:call-template` element to do so. As you know from Chapter 3, "Branching & Control Functions," the basic format of `xsl:call-template` is:

```
<xsl:call-template name="template_name" />
```

where *template_name* is the name of the template you want to invoke. This format doesn't work in this case, however. Because you need to define `xsl:with-param` elements as content of the `xsl:call-template`, you must define the element with opening and closing tags, as in:

```
<xsl:call-template name="template_name">
...
</xsl:call-template>
```

Once you do this, you can specify the parameters and parameter values you want to pass to the template. In the following example, you pass width and height parameter values to the SquareOrRectangleArea template:

```
<xsl:call-template name="SquareOrRectangleArea">
   <xsl:with-param name="width" select="10"/>
   <xsl:with-param name="height" select="20/>
</xsl:call-template>
```

The resulting output from this template call is:

```
200
```

To pass a parameter value to a template, follow these steps:

1. Modify the `xsl:call-template` or `xsl:apply-templates` element so that it has an opening and closing tag, such as **<xsl:call-template name="myTemplate"> </xsl:call-template>**.
2. Insert the following as the contents of the `xsl:call-template` or `xsl:apply-templates` element: **<xsl:with-param name="*parameter_name*" select="*parameter_value*" />**, where *parameter_name* is the name of the parameter you previously defined and *parameter_value* is an optional value that you want to pass to this parameter.

Note If you don't pass a specific value, the default value for the parameter is used. If there's no default value, an empty string ("") is used.

Using Global Parameters

So far you've worked only with local parameters that were defined and used with specific templates. XSLT defines another type of parameter called a global parameter, which can be referenced anywhere in an XSLT stylesheet once it's defined. A global parameter is simply a parameter that's defined at the top level of the stylesheet. That is, the parameter is defined as a child of the `xsl:stylesheet` element in the same way you define `xsl:template` elements as children of the `xsl:stylesheet` element. Here's an example:

```
<xsl:stylesheet version="2.0"
  xmlns:xsl="http://www.w3.org/1999/XSL/Transform">

<xsl:output method="html"/>

<xsl:param name="textColor"/>
<xsl:param name="pageBGColor"/>
<xsl:param name="tableBGColor"/>

<xsl:template match="/">
    <html>
      <body bgcolor="{$pageBGColor}" text="{$textColor}">
        <table bgcolor="{$tableBGColor}">
            <tr>
                <th>Inv Number</th>
                <th>Item</th>
                <th>Manufacturer</th>
                <th>Current</th>
                <th>Orders</th>
                <th>Remaining</th>
            </tr>
            <xsl:for-each select="inventory/item"/>
            <tr>
                <td><xsl:value-of
select="@tracking_number"/></td>
                <td><xsl:value-of select="item_type"/></td>
                <td><xsl:value-of
select="@manufacturer"/></td>
```

```
                <td><xsl:value-of
select="stock/@in_stock"/></td>
                <td><xsl:value-of
select="stock/@orders_for"/></td>
                <td><xsl:value-of
select="stock/@net_units"/></td>
              </tr>
            </xsl:for-each>
        </table>
      </body>
    </html>
</xsl:template>

</xsl:stylesheet>
```

Here, you define three global parameters: textColor, pageBGColor, and tableBGColor. You then use the parameter values to set attributes of the <body> and <table> tags in the HTML output.

You set the value of global parameters in one of two ways. You can set a default value directly when you define the parameter, such as:

```
<xsl:param name="textColor">
   <xsl:text>black</xsl:text>
</xsl:param>
<xsl:param name="pageBGColor">
   <xsl:text>white</xsl:text>
</xsl:param>
<xsl:param name="tableBGColor">
   <xsl:text>blue</xsl:text>
</xsl:param>
```

and

```
<xsl:param name="textColor" select='black'" />
<xsl:param name="pageBGColor" select='white'" />
<xsl:param name="tableBGColor" select='blue'" />
```

Alternatively, you can set the value of the global parameter when you invoke the XSLT processor. You specify global variable values as command line arguments:

```
java org.apache.xalan.xslt.Process -in file_in -xsl file_xsl
 -out file_out -param param1 value1 -param param2 value2
 -param paramN valueN
```

where *file_in* is the input XML document, *file_xsl* is the XSL stylesheet, *file_out* is the output file, and each –param flag is followed by a global parameter name and value, such as:

```
java org.apache.xalan.xslt.Process -in sample.xml -xsl
sample.xsl
 -out sample.html -param textColor black -param pageBGColor
white
 -param tableBGColor blue
```

XSLT processors are usually invoked from within application programs rather than from the command line. For example, if the XSLT processor you're using supports the Transformation API for XML (TrAX), you could define the global parameters prior to calling the methods that parse and process the contents of the input XML document. With TrAX, you do this using the setParameter method of the Transformer classes that you're using to handle the input stream, which represents the input XML document you're using as the source document, and the Java source code to do this would look like this:

```
import java.io.File;
import javax.xml.transform.Transformer;
import javax.xml.transform.TransformerConfigurationException;
import javax.xml.transform.TransformerException;
import javax.xml.transform.TransformerFactory;
import javax.xml.transform.stream.StreamResult;
import javax.xml.transform.stream.StreamSource;

public class DefineGPs {

  public static void parseAndProcess(String sourceID, String
xslID,
                                     String outputID) {
```

```
    try {

      TransformerFactory trfactory =
TransformerFactory.newInstance();

      Transformer transformer =
        trfactory.newTransformer(new StreamSource(xslID));
      transformer.setParameter("textColor", "black");
      transformer.setParameter("pageBGColor", "white");
      transformer.setParameter("tableBGColor", "blue");

      transformer.transform(new StreamSource(new
File(sourceID)),
                                new StreamResult(new
File(outputID)));
    }

    catch (TransformerConfigurationException trce) {
    }
    catch (TransformerException tre) {
    }
  }

  public static void main(String argv[])
     throws java.io.IOException, org.xml.sax.SAXException {

    DefineGPs gps = new DefineGPs();
    gps.parseAndProcess("sample.xml", "sample.xsl",
"sample.html");

  }
}
```

Essentially, this source code is the equivalent of the previously defined command line instruction for the XSLT processor. You set the global parameters textColor, pageBGColor, and tableBGColor to black, white, and blue respectively, and then you specify that the input (or source) document as sample.xml, the XSLT stylesheet as sample.xsl, and the output document as sample.html. Thus, if the input document looked like this:

```
<?xml version="1.0" ?>
<inventory>
   <item tracking_number="459320" manufacturer="MHWB
Industries">
      <item_type>Fiberglass Prehung Entry Door</item_type>
      <description>6-panel left-hand inswing entry door,
primed, white</description>
      <stock in_stock="750" orders_for="200" net_units="550"
order="N" />
   </item>
   <item tracking_number="459323" manufacturer="Not listed">
      <item_type>Fiberglass Prehung Entry Door</item_type>
      <description>6-panel left-hand inswing entry door,
primed, white</description>
      <stock in_stock="50" orders_for="200" net_units="-150"
order="Y" />
   </item>
   <item tracking_number="459780" manufacturer="MHWB
Industries">
      <item_type>Steel Prehung Entry Door</item_type>
      <description>4-panel left-hand inswing entry door,
primed, black, steel</description>
      <stock in_stock="250" orders_for="200" net_units="50"
order="Y" />
   </item>
   <item tracking_number="459789" manufacturer="Not listed">
      <item_type>Steel Prehung Entry Door</item_type>
      <description>4-panel left-hand inswing entry door,
primed, black, steel</description>
      <stock in_stock="0" orders_for="200" net_units="-200"
order="Y" />
   </item>
</inventory>
```

and the stylesheet was the one previously defined in this section, the output document would look similar to this:

```
<html>
  <body bgcolor="black" text="white">
    <table bgcolor="blue">
      <tr>
        <th>Inv Number</th>
        <th>Item</th>
        <th>Manufacturer</th>
        <th>Current</th>
        <th>Orders</th>
        <th>Remaining</th>
      </tr>
      <tr>
         <td>459320</td>
         <td>Fiberglass Prehung Entry Door</td>
         <td>MHWB Industries</td>
         <td>750</td>
         <td>200</td>
         <td>550</td>
       </tr>
      <tr>
         <td>459323</td>
         <td>Fiberglass Prehung Entry Door</td>
         <td>Not listed</td>
         <td>50</td>
         <td>200</td>
         <td>-150</td>
       </tr>
      <tr>
         <td>459780</td>
         <td>Steel Prehung Entry Door</td>
         <td>MHWB Industries</td>
         <td>250</td>
         <td>200</td>
         <td>50</td>
       </tr>
      <tr>
         <td>459789</td>
```

```
            <td>Steel Prehung Entry Door</td>
            <td>Not listed</td>
            <td>0</td>
            <td>200</td>
            <td>-200</td>
        </tr>
    </table>
  </body>
</html>
```

To define a global parameter with a simple default value or no default value, follow these steps:

1. Immediately after the opening stylesheet tag <xsl:stylesheet> and any `xsl:include` or `xsl:import` declarations, type **<xsl:param name="*parameter_name*"**, where *parameter_name* is the name you want to use for the global parameter.
2. If you want to set a default value for the parameter, type **select="*parameter_value*"/>**, where parameter_value is the default value you want to assign to the parameter. Otherwise, type **/>**.

To define a global parameter with default contents, follow these steps:

1. Immediately after the opening stylesheet tag <xsl:stylesheet> and any `xsl:include` or `xsl:import` declarations, type **<xsl:param name="*parameter_name*">**, where *parameter_name* is the name you want to use for the parameter.
2. Insert the contents of the parameter.
3. Type **</xsl:parameter>** to complete the parameter declaration.

To reference a global parameter, follow these steps:

1. If the global parameter is used as part of the XSLT markup, type **$*parameter_name***, where *parameter_name* is the name of the parameter you previously defined and want to use.
2. If the parameter is used as part of the attribute in the output, type **{$*parameter_name*}**, where *parameter_name* is the name of the parameter you previously defined and want to use.

To pass a global parameter value to a template, follow these steps:

1. Modify the `xsl:call-template` or `xsl:apply-templates` element so that it has an opening and closing tag, such as <xsl:call-template name="myTemplate"> </xsl:call-template>.
2. As the contents of the `xsl:call-template` or `xsl:apply-templates` element, enter **<xsl:with-param name="*parameter_name*" select="*parameter_value*" />**, where *parameter_name* is the name of the parameter you previously defined and *parameter_value* is an optional value that you want to pass to this parameter.

Note If you don't pass a specific value, the default value for the global parameter is used. If there's no default value, an empty string ("") is used.

Working with Variables

When you're working with XSLT, you'll often need a way to hold values temporarily during processing, and this is where you'll find that variables are extremely useful. You use variables to store values.

Defining Variables

Variables are defined using the `xsl:variable` element, which has the basic form:

```
<xsl:variable name="variable_name" select="variable_value" />
```

where *variable_name* is the name of the variable you're defining and *variable_value* is the value you're assigning to the variable. As with parameters, the select attribute that sets a value is optional. If you don't set a specific value, the XSLT processor assigns an empty string ("") as the default value.

This means you could define a variable called statusFlag that has the value true, like this:

```
<xsl:variable name="statusFlag" select="'true'" />
```

Note As with parameters, you must use single quotation marks to enclose literal string values. If you don't, the XSLT processor assumes you're referencing an element name.

Variables can have contents as well. This means you could also specify a literal string value for the statusFlag variable like this:

```
<xsl:variable name="statusFlag">
  <xsl:text>true</xsl:text>
</xsl:variable>
```

However, if you wanted to initialize the same variable to an empty string, you'd declare the variable like this:

```
<xsl:variable name="statusFlag"/>
```

Now statusFlag has the value "".

You can use variables in XSLT in much the same way that you can use them in programming languages. For example, if you needed to implement the following Java code in XSLT:

```
int x;
if (statusFlag > 0)
   x = 5;
else
   x = 0;
```

you could do this using the following variable declaration:

```
<xsl:variable name="x"/>
  <xsl:choose>
    <xsl:when test="$statusFlag &gt; 0">
      <xsl:text>5</xsl:text>
```

```
      </xsl:when>
      <xsl:otherwise>
        <xsl:text>0</xsl:text>
      </xsl:otherwise>
    </xsl:choose>
</xsl:variable>
```

Unlike traditional programming languages, however, where you can modify the value of a variable during execution and reassign the value to the variable to modify further execution, you can't do this in XSLT. XSLT doesn't execute stylesheets—it processes them recursively or iteratively. For example, in Java you can reassign values to variables using statements like this:

```
x+=1
++x
x++
```

In Java, reassigning the value of a variable allows the language to be very dynamic. Consider the following assignments:

```
a=2;
b=++a
```

Here, the result is that the value of a is 3 and the value of b is 3. Yet if you rewrite the assignments like this:

```
a=2;
b=a++
```

The result is that the value of a is 3 and the value of b is 2.

Although Java has these types of reassignments, many less complex programming languages do not. The reason is that value reassignments are difficult to implement and track. Suffice it to say that the designers of XSLT chose not to open this Pandora's box when they defined the specification.

To define a variable with a simple default value or no default value, follow these steps:

1. Within the template that you want to define the variable, type **<xsl:variable name="*variable_name*"**, where *variable_name* is the name you want to use for the variable.
2. If you want to set a default value for the variable, type **select="*variable_value*"/>**, where variable_value is the default value you want to assign to the variable. Otherwise, type **/>**.

To define a variable with default contents, follow these steps:

1. Within the template that you want to define the variable, type **<xsl:variable name="*variable_name*">**, where *variable_name* is the name you want to use for the variable.
2. Insert the contents of the variable.
3. Type **</xsl:variable>** to complete the variable declaration.

Referencing Variables

You reference variables in the same way you reference parameters. This means a variable reference has the form:

$variable_name

where *variable_name* is the name of the variable you've defined and want to use. As long as you reference the variable as part of an XSLT element's attribute or text, you can use this basic syntax. Here's an example:

```
<xsl:template match="/">
    <html>
      <body>
        <xsl:apply-templates select="inventory/item"/>
      </body>
    </html>
</xsl:template>

<xsl:template match="item">
  <xsl:choose>
    <xsl:when test="$statusFlag = 0">
      <p>Please order, stock number:
```

```
      <xsl:value-of select="@tracking_number"/>
     </p>
    </xsl:when>
    <xsl:when test="$statusFlag = 1">
      <p>Item <xsl:value-of select="@tracking_number"/>
      doesn't need to be re-stocked at this time.</p>
    </xsl:when>
    <xsl:otherwise>
      <p>INVALID ORDER INDICATOR FOR ITEM:
      <xsl:value-of select="@tracking_number"/>
      </p>
    </xsl:otherwise >
  </xsl:choose>
</xsl:template>
```

In this example a variable called statusFlag is used to determine whether items should be ordered. If statusFlag is set to 0, the item should be ordered. If statusFlag is set to 1, the item doesn't need to be ordered. If statusFlag has a different value, some error occurred during processing and you should check the item order status.

If you want to reference variables in attributes that you want to generate as part of the output markup, you must enclose the variable reference in curly braces, such as:

```
{$variable_name}
```

As with parameters, the curly braces tell the XSLT processor to replace the referenced value with its actual value.

To reference a variable, follow these steps:

1. If the variable is used as part of the XSLT markup, type ***$variable_name***, where *variable_name* is the name of the variable you previously defined and want to use.
2. If the variable is used as part of the attribute in the output, type **{*$variable_name*}**, where *variable_name* is the name of the variable you previously defined and want to use.

Using Global Variables

Like parameters, variables can have a global or local scope. You define global variables at the top level of the stylesheet and their values are accessible anywhere in the stylesheet. On the other hand, you define local variables as part of a specific template and their values are only available in that template.

The following example defines four global variables (statusFlag, x, y, and z):

```
<xsl:stylesheet version="2.0"
  xmlns:xsl="http://www.w3.org/1999/XSL/Transform">

<xsl:output method="html"/>

<xsl:variable name="statusFlag"/>
<xsl:variable name="x"/>
<xsl:variable name="y"/>
<xsl:variable name="z"/>

<xsl:template match="/">
...
</xsl:template">

</xsl:stylesheet>
```

Caution If you define a local variable with the same name as a global variable, the local variable overrides the global variable. This means that the value of the local variable is used instead of the global variable with the same name.

To define a global variable with a simple default value or no default value, follow these steps:

1. After the opening stylesheet tag <xsl:stylesheet> and any `xsl:include`, `xsl:import`, or `xsl:param` declarations, type **<xsl:variable**

name="*variable_name*", where *variable_name* is the name you want to use for the global variable.

2. If you want to set a default value for the variable, type **select="*variable_value*"/>**, where *variable_value* is the default value you want to assign to the variable. Otherwise, type **/>**.

To define a global variable with default contents, follow these steps:

1. Immediately after the opening stylesheet tag <xsl:stylesheet>, and any `xsl:include`, `xsl:import`, or `xsl:param` declarations, type **<xsl:variable name="*variable_name*">**, where *variable_name* is the name you want to use for the variable.
2. Insert the contents of the variable.
3. Type **</xsl:variable>** to complete the variable declaration.

To reference a global variable, follow these steps:

1. If the global variable is used as part of the XSLT markup, type **$*variable_name***, where *variable_name* is the name of the variable you previously defined and want to use.
2. If the variable is used as part of the attribute in the output, type **{$*variable_name*}**, where *variable_name* is the name of the variable you previously defined and want to use.

Chapter 5. Working with Strings, Booleans, & Numbers

Previous chapters have discussed strings, Booleans, and numbers, but they haven't really discussed in detail how to manipulate these datatypes. This chapter fills that gap by explaining how to work with strings, Booleans, and numbers. Although the emphasis is on converting, sorting, extracting, and merging strings, you'll also learn how to how to format numbers and how to get the most out of Booleans.

Manipulating Strings

XSL Transformations (XSLT) and XML Path (XPath) define many functions for working with string values. You can use these functions to

- Convert numeric and Boolean values to strings
- Manage spaces within strings
- Sort and merge strings
- Extract substrings from strings
- Translate individual characters in strings

Converting Values to Strings

You use the string() function to convert selected values to strings. You can also use the string() function to convert parameter and variable values to strings.

Table 5-1 provides a summary of the string conversion rules for various types of values. As the table shows, Boolean values, integers, floats, special numeric values, and node sets are all converted in different ways.

Table 5-1 Value Conversion to Strings

VALUE TYPE	CONVERSION DESCRIPTION
Boolean	Boolean values `true` and `false` are converted to the strings "true" and "false", respectively. Example: "true"
Integer	Converted to a string representing the integer. The value won't have a decimal point or leading zeroes. If the integer is negative, it'll be preceded by a minus sign (-). Example: "-252"
Floating point	Converted to a string with at least one number before the decimal point and one number after the decimal point. If a number only has a fractional component, a zero is used to left of the decimal point. This is only time a leading zero occurs before the decimal point. Example: "0.5254245"
Special numeric values	Positive zero, negative zero, positive infinity, negative infinity, and NaN ("not a number") are converted to string representations. Examples: 0 becomes "0" -0 becomes "0" INF becomes "Infinity" -INF becomes "-Infinity" NaN becomes "NaN"
Node set	Only the first node in a node set is converted to a string representation. Node order is determined by the order nodes are in the original document . Example: The first node is the node that appears prior to other nodes in the document.

Most of the time the XSLT processor will perform string conversions for you behind the scenes. For example, you can specify that you want to select the current node and output its contents like this:

```
<xsl:value-of select="."/>
```

or you can explicitly convert the node's contents to a string like this:

```
<xsl:value-of select="string(.)"/>
```

The string() function can be useful when you're performing calculations and the result might not be a number. In this case, you might want to convert the result to a string before outputting it, such as:

```
<xsl:template name="CircleArea">
   <xsl:param name="circumference"/>
   <xsl:param name="diameter"/>
   <text>The area of the circle is: </text>
   <xsl:value-of select="string($circumference * $diameter)"/>
</xsl:template>
```

Here, you convert the product of the circumference and diameter parameters to a string value.

To convert a value to a string:

- As part of a select attribute or within another function, type **string(*expression*)**, where *expression* is an XPath expression that returns a node set or an actual value that you want to convert to a string.

Managing Spaces Within Strings

If you need to manage spaces within strings or the contents of a node, you'll find that `xsl:preserve-space` and `xsl:strip-space` are useful. `xsl:preserve-space` is a top-level element that specifies a list of elements for which whitespace should be preserved. `xsl:strip-space` is a top-level element that specifies a list of elements for which whitespace should be removed.

The `xsl:preserve-space` and `xsl:strip-space` elements have nearly identical syntax. The basic form for `xsl:preserve-space` is:

```
<xsl:preserve-space elements="element1 element2 … elementN" />
```

The basic form for `xsl:strip-space` is:

```
<xsl:strip-space elements="element1 element2 … elementN" />
```

Both elements are always used as empty elements and their elements attribute is required.

> **Tip** Technically, the value of the `elements` attribute for `xsl:preserve-space` and `xsl:strip-space` match element names as an XPath expression. With this in mind, you could specify elements="*" to match all element names.

The key thing to keep in mind when working with `xsl:preserve-space` and `xsl:strip-space` is that they don't preserve or strip all whitespace. Instead, they preserve or strip nonsignificant whitespace. Nonsignificant whitespace refers to whitespace that occurs in and around elements or is the only contents of an element's text node. In the following example, the nonsignificant whitespace for the data element is the spaces between the child elements `h` and `d`:

```
<document>
 <data>
  <h>Manufacturer</h>  <d>MHWB Industries</d>
  <h>Inventory #</h>  <d>459320</d>
  <h>Item</h>  <d>Fiberglass Prehung Entry Door</d>
  <h>Orders</h>  <d>308</d>
 </data>
</document>
```

If you wanted to preserve the nonsignificant whitespace in the document to achieve output like this:

```
Manufacturer  MHWB Industries
Inventory #  459320
Item  Fiberglass Prehung Entry Door
Orders  308
```

you'd have to define the XSLT stylesheet so that nonsignificant whitespace is preserved for the data element. Here's an example:

```
<?xml version="1.0"?>
<xsl:stylesheet version="1.0"
     xmlns:xsl="http://www.w3.org/1999/XSL/Transform">

  <xsl:output method="text"/>
  <xsl:preserve-space elements="data"/>

  <xsl:template match="/">
    <xsl:for-each select="/document/data">
      <xsl:value-of select="."/>
    </xsl:for-each>
  </xsl:template>

</xsl:stylesheet>
```

On the other hand, if the input data looked like this:

```
<document>
 <data>
  <h>Manufacturer:</h>  <d>MHWB Industries</d>
  <h>Inventory #</h>  <d>459320</d>
  <h>Item:</h>  <d>Fiberglass Prehung Entry Door</d>
  <h>Orders:</h>  <d>308</d>
 </data>
</document>
```

and you wanted the output to look like this:

```
Manufacturer:MHWB Industries
Inventory #459320
```

```
Item:Fiberglass Prehung Entry Door
Orders:308
```

you could ensure that the nonsignificant spaces weren't used by defining the stylesheet like this:

```
<?xml version="1.0"?>
<xsl:stylesheet version="2.0"
  xmlns:xsl="http://www.w3.org/1999/XSL/Transform">

  <xsl:output method="text"/>
  <xsl:strip-space elements="data"/>

  <xsl:template match="/">
    <xsl:for-each select="/document/data">
      <xsl:value-of select="."/>
    </xsl:for-each>
  </xsl:template>

</xsl:stylesheet>
```

If you want to manage the use of nonsignificant whitespace, follow these steps:

1. As noted previously, define the `xsl:preserve-space` and `xsl:strip-space` elements at the top level of the stylesheet. They don't, however, need to immediately follow the opening <xsl:stylesheet> tag.
2. To preserve nonsignificant whitespace for an element or a group of elements, type **<xsl:preserve-space elements="*element1 element2 ... elementN*" />**, where *element1 element2 ... elementN* is a space-separated list of elements whose nonsignificant whitespace should be preserved. Or type **<xsl:preserve-space elements="*" />** to preserve nonsignificant whitespace for all elements.
3. To strip nonsignificant whitespace for an element or a group of elements, type **<xsl:strip-space elements="*element1 element2 ... elementN*" />**, where *element1 element2 ... elementN* is a space-separated list of elements whose nonsignificant whitespace should be stripped. Or type **<xsl:strip-space elements="*" />** to strip nonsignificant whitespace for all elements.

Note You can't specify the same list of elements to strip or preserve. This list must be different.

Normalizing Space in Strings

Another useful structure for managing spaces within strings is the normalize_space() function. In XSLT a normalized string is similar to a token in XML Schema. This means that the normalize-space() function removes carriage returns, line feeds, tabs, leading spaces, and trailing spaces and replaces multiple occurrences of the space character with a single space anywhere they occur within the string.

To see how the normalize-space() function works, consider the following example stylesheet:

```
<?xml version="1.0"?>
<xsl:stylesheet version="2.0"
  xmlns:xsl="http://www.w3.org/1999/XSL/Transform">

  <xsl:output method="text"/>

  <xsl:variable name="theString">
    <xsl:text>                This string
has
way
      too
      much
      whitespace.
    </xsl:text>
  </xsl:variable>

  <xsl:template match="/">
    <xsl:value-of select="normalize-space($theString)"/>
  </xsl:template>
```

```
</xsl:stylesheet>
```

The output of this stylesheet is:

```
This string has way too much whitespace.
```

To normalize a string, do the following

- As part of a select attribute or within another function, type **normalize-space(*expression*)**, where *expression* is an XPath expression that returns a node set or an actual value that you want to convert to a string and normalize.

Merging Values into a Single String

If you need to merge multiple values into a single string, you can do this using the concat() function. Any values that you merge that aren't strings are converted to strings as if you had processed them with the string() function.

The basic format of the contact function is:

```
concat(value1, value2, …, valueN)
```

where *value1*, *value2*, …, *valueN* are the values you want to concatenate.

Let's say you wanted to output a list of file names in the format filename.ext where the filename came from one variable and the extension came from a different variable. To get these values to output as a filename, you could specify:

```
<xsl:value-of select="concat($file_name,'.',$file_ext)"/>
```

Thus, if the file_name variable has the value "data_source" and the file_ext variable has the value "xml", the output is the concatenated string:

```
data_source.xml
```

To merge string values, do the following:

- As part of a select attribute or within another function, type **concat(value1, value2, ..., valueN)**, where *value1*, *value2*, ..., *valueN* are the values you want to concatenate.

Examining and Manipulating String Contents

XSLT and XPath provide several functions you can use to examine the contents of strings. Table 5-2 provides a summary of the key functions.

Table 5-2. String Manipulation Functions

FUNCTION	DESCRIPTION
contains()	Determines if the first string contains the second string. Returns true if the first string contains the second. Otherwise, returns false. Syntax: contains(string1, string2)
string-length()	Determines the number of characters in the referenced string. If no string is passed to the function, the function converts the context node to a string and returns the length of that string. Returns the number of characters in the string or context node. Syntax: string-length(string)
starts-with()	Determines if the first string begins with the second string. Returns true if the first string starts with the second. Otherwise, returns false. Syntax: starts-with(string1, string2)
substring()	Extracts a portion of a string. The function accepts three arguments: the string you want to work with, the position of the first character of the substring, and an optional number of characters from the position specified to return. Syntax: substring(string, sub_position, num_chars?)
substring-	Searches for a substring within a string and returns the

after()	characters that occur after the substring. Syntax: substring-after(orig_string, search_string)
substring-before()	Searches for a substring within a string and returns the characters that occur before the substring. Syntax: substring-before(orig_string, search_string)

Essentially, these utility functions examine an input string, which could be the contents of a node specified with an XPath expression, and do something with it, such as determining the string's length and displaying this to the output. To see how these functions work, consider the following input document:

```
<accounts>
  <customer>11285:William Stanek</customer>
  <customer>10487:William R. Stanek, Sr.</customer>
  <customer>09685:Robert W. Stanek</customer>
</accounts>
```

If you wanted to examine the contents of the `customer` element, you could work with this content in a number of ways. With string-length(), you could examine the number of characters in each `customer` element, such as:

```
  <xsl:variable name="newline">
<xsl:text>
</xsl:text>
  </xsl:variable>

<xsl:template match="/">
  <xsl:for-each select="customer">
    <xsl:text>String #</xsl:text>
    <xsl:value-of select="position()"/>
    <xsl:text> has length: </xsl:text>
    <xsl:value-of select="string-length(.)"/>
    <xsl:text>.</xsl:text>
```

```
    <xsl:value-of select="$newline"/>
  </xsl:for-each>
</xsl:template>
```

The output would look like this:

```
String #1 has length: 21.
String #2 has length: 29.
String #3 has length: 23.
```

Using starts-with, you could search for a particular value at the beginning of the element contents and then return the entire contents of the matching element. Here's an example:

```
<xsl:template match="/">
  <xsl:for-each select="customer">
    <xsl:value-of select="starts-with(., '10487')"/>
    <xsl:text>.</xsl:text>
    <xsl:value-of select="$newline"/>
  </xsl:for-each>
</xsl:template>
```

Using the previously defined input document, this template outputs:

```
10487:William R. Stanek, Sr.
```

If you want to see only account numbers, you could extract a substring from the element contents. Since the account number starts at position 1 and contains five characters, a template rule that extracted this information would look like this:

```
<xsl:template match="/">
  <xsl:for-each select="customer">
    <xsl:value-of select="substring(.,1,5)"/>
    <xsl:text>.</xsl:text>
    <xsl:value-of select="$newline"/>
  </xsl:for-each>
</xsl:template>
```

Now the output is:

```
11285
10487
09685
```

If you wanted only the account names instead of the account numbers, you could specify the substring that started in the sixth character position and then not specify the number of characters to return. Essentially, this declaration would say: return all characters after the fifth character in the string. The template rule to perform this task is:

```
<xsl:template match="/">
  <xsl:for-each select="customer">
    <xsl:value-of select="substring(.,6)"/>
    <xsl:text>.</xsl:text>
    <xsl:value-of select="$newline"/>
  </xsl:for-each>
</xsl:template>
```

The output is now:

```
William Stanek
William R. Stanek, Sr.
Robert W. Stanek
```

Because there's always another way of doing things in XSLT, you could have also used substring-before() and substring-after() to perform these tasks. Here, if you returned the substring before the first occurrence of :, you'd get the account number:

```
<xsl:template match="/">
  <xsl:for-each select="customer">
    <xsl:value-of select="substring-before(.,':')"/>
    <xsl:text>.</xsl:text>
    <xsl:value-of select="$newline"/>
  </xsl:for-each>
</xsl:template>
```

And if you returned the substring after the first occurrence of :, you'd get the account name:

```
<xsl:template match="/">
  <xsl:for-each select="customer">
    <xsl:value-of select="substring-after(.,':')"/>
    <xsl:text>.</xsl:text>
    <xsl:value-of select="$newline"/>
  </xsl:for-each>
</xsl:template>
```

To see how multiple string manipulation functions could be used together, consider the following example that implements a search and replace function using contains(), substring-before(), and substring-after():

```
<xsl:stylesheet version="2.0"
  xmlns:xsl="http://www.w3.org/1999/XSL/Transform">

  <xsl:output method="text"/>

  <xsl:template match="/">
    <xsl:variable name="test">
      <xsl:call-template name="search_replace_string">
        <xsl:with-param name="orig_string">
          <xsl:value-of select="customer"/>
        </xsl:with-param>
        <xsl:with-param name="substring">
            <xsl:text>:</xsl:text>
        </xsl:with-param>
        <xsl:with-param name="replace_string">
            <xsl:text>:</xsl:text>
        </xsl:with-param>
      </xsl:call-template>
    </xsl:variable>
    <xsl:value-of select="$test"/>
  </xsl:template>

  <xsl:template name="search_replace_string">
    <xsl:param name="orig_string"/>
    <xsl:param name="substring"/>
```

```
<xsl:param name="replace_string" select="''"/>
<xsl:variable name="beg_string">
  <xsl:choose>
    <xsl:when test="contains($orig_string, $substring)">
      <xsl:value-of select="substring-before($orig_string,
                              $substring)"/>
    </xsl:when>
    <xsl:otherwise>
      <xsl:value-of select="$orig_string"/>
    </xsl:otherwise>
  </xsl:choose>
</xsl:variable>
<xsl:variable name="mid_string">
  <xsl:choose>
    <xsl:when test="contains($orig_string, $substring)">
      <xsl:value-of select="$replace_string"/>
    </xsl:when>
    <xsl:otherwise>
      <xsl:text></xsl:text>
    </xsl:otherwise>
  </xsl:choose>
</xsl:variable>
<xsl:variable name="end_string">
  <xsl:choose>
    <xsl:when test="contains($orig_string, $substring)">
      <xsl:choose>
        <xsl:when test="contains(substring-
after($orig_string,
                        $substring), $substring)">
          <xsl:call-template name="search_replace_string">
            <xsl:with-param name="orig_string">
              <xsl:value-of select="substring-
after($orig_string,
                                  $substring)"/>
            </xsl:with-param>
            <xsl:with-param name="substring">
              <xsl:value-of select="$substring"/>
            </xsl:with-param>
```

```
                <xsl:with-param name="replace_string">
                  <xsl:value-of select="$replace_string"/>
                </xsl:with-param>
              </xsl:call-template>
            </xsl:when>
            <xsl:otherwise>
              <xsl:value-of select="substring-
after($orig_string,
                                            $substring)"/>
            </xsl:otherwise>
          </xsl:choose>
        </xsl:when>
        <xsl:otherwise>
          <xsl:text></xsl:text>
        </xsl:otherwise>
      </xsl:choose>
    </xsl:variable>
    <xsl:value-of select="concat($beg_string, $mid_string,
$end_string)"/>
  </xsl:template>

</xsl:stylesheet>
```

In this example, you define the element you want to search as the customer element, the substring you want to replace as ":", and the replacement text as a space. The result is a reformatting of the output. Instead of:

```
11285:William Stanek
10487:William R. Stanek, Sr.
09685:Robert W. Stanek
```

the output becomes:

```
11285 William Stanek
10487 William R. Stanek, Sr.
09685 Robert W. Stanek
```

The search and replace function allows you to search and replace any string value. For example, if you needed to replace occurrences of "Robert W." with "William R.", you could have done this as well. You'd make those changes in the root template like this:

```
<xsl:template match="/">
  <xsl:variable name="test">
    <xsl:call-template name="search_replace_string">
      <xsl:with-param name="orig_string">
        <xsl:value-of select="customer"/>
      </xsl:with-param>
      <xsl:with-param name="substring">
          <xsl:text>Robert W.</xsl:text>
      </xsl:with-param>
      <xsl:with-param name="replace_string">
          <xsl:text>William R.</xsl:text>
      </xsl:with-param>
    </xsl:call-template>
  </xsl:variable>
  <xsl:value-of select="$test"/>
</xsl:template>
```

Determining If a String Contains Another String

You use the contains() function to determine if a string contains another string. You can use the contains() function in your stylesheet by following these steps:

1. As part of a select attribute or within another function, type **contains(*string1*, *string2*)**, where *string1* is the string you want to examine and *string2* is the string you want to search for.
2. The function returns true if the first string contains the second. Otherwise, the function returns false.

Determining String Length

You use the string-length() function to determine the number of characters in the referenced string. You can use the string-length() function in your stylesheet by following these steps:

1. As part of a select attribute or within another function, type **string-**

length(*string*), where *string* is the string you want to examine.

2. The function returns the number of characters. If no string is passed to the function, the function converts the context node to a string and returns the length of that string.

Determining If a String Starts with Another String

You use the starts-with() function to determine if a string begins with another string. You can use the starts-with() function in your stylesheet by following these steps:

1. As part of a select attribute or within another function, type **starts-with(*string1*, *string2*)**, where *string1* is the string you want to examine and *string2* is the string you want to search for at the beginning of the first string.
2. The function returns true if the first string starts with the second. Otherwise, the function returns false.

Extracting a Substring

You use the substring() function to extract of portion of a string. You can use the substring() function in your stylesheet by following these steps:

1. As part of a select attribute or within another function, type **substring(*string*, *sub_position*, *num_chars?*)**, where *string* is the string you want to work with, *sub_position* is the position of the first character of the substring, and *num_chars* is the optional number of characters from the position specified to return.
2. The function returns the substring starting at the position specified to the end of the string or to the number of characters specified.

Note The position of the first character in a string is 1, which is different from many programming languages where the position of the first character in a string is 0.

Returning a Substring Before Another String

You use the substring-before() function to return the portion of a string that occurs before a specific substring. You can use the substring-before() function in your stylesheet by following these steps:

1. As part of a select attribute or within another function, type **substring-before(*orig_string, search_string*)**, where *orig_string* is the string you want to work with and *search_string* is the substring that you want to find within the original string.
2. The function returns the characters that occur after the specified substring. If the substring isn't found, an empty string is returned.

Returning a Substring After Another String

You use the substring-after() function to return the portion of a string that occurs after a specific substring. You can use the substring-after() function in your stylesheet by following these steps:

1. As part of a select attribute or within another function, type **substring-after(*orig_string, search_string*)**, where *orig_string* is the string you want to work with and *search_string* is the substring that you want to find within the original string.
2. The function returns the characters that occur after the specified substring. If the substring isn't found, an empty string is returned.

Translating Characters in Strings

Not only can you implement search and replace functions in XSLT, you can also convert individual characters in strings. The function you use to convert characters within strings is called translate(). This function has the basic form:

```
translate(input_string, chars_to_convert, output_chars)
```

where *input_string* is an actual string of the contents of a node specified with an XPath expression, *chars_to_convert* defines the characters in the input string that you want to convert, and *output_chars* defines the new character format.

Believe me, this makes much more sense when you see the translate() function in action. Consider the following example:

```
<xsl:value-of select="translate(.,
'abcdefghijklmnopqrstuvwxyz',

'ABCDEFGHIJKLMNOPQRSTUVWXYZ')"/>
```

This declaration says to use contents of the context node as the input string and convert any lowercase letters in those contents to an uppercase letter. Thus, if the input element looked like this:

```
<customer>10487:William R. Stanek, Sr.</customer>
```

The output would be:

```
10487:WILLIAM R. STANEK, SR.
```

Characters defined in the *chars_to_convert* string are compared on a character-by-character basis and matched to characters in the *output_chars* string. This means the character in the first position of the *chars_to_convert* string is matched to the first character in the *output_chars* string, the character in the second position of the *chars_to_convert* string is matched to the second character in the *output_chars* string, and so on.

Tip The value of characters in a specific position doesn't matter to the XSLT processor. The XSLT processor doesn't understand plain language as you and I do. If you had said to match "ABC" with "XYZ", the XSLT processor would have done this, meaning all capital A's in the input string would be translated to capital X's, capital B's to capital Y's, and capital C's to capital Z's.

If you want to translate characters on a character-by-character basis, the *output_chars* string should be as long as the *chars_to_convert* string. If the *chars_to_convert* string is longer than the *output_chars* string, there will be no translation values for some characters. As a result, the values will be omitted. Although this could cause problems in your translations, this behavior can also be useful. For example, if you wanted to remove punctuation marks (periods, colons, commas, and semicolons) from input, you could specify the following translation:

```
<xsl:value-of select="translate(., ';:.,', '')"/>
```

This translation says to replace any occurrences of ;, :, ., or , but doesn't provide a translation. As a result, the characters are omitted in the output string.

You use the translation() function in your stylesheet by following these steps:

1. As part of a select attribute or within another function, type **translate(*input_string, chars_to_convert, output_chars*)**, where *input_string* is an actual string of the contents of a node specified with an XPath expression, *chars_to_convert* defines the characters in the input string that you want to convert, and *output_chars* defines the new character format.
2. Characters are compared on a character-by-character basis. This means the character in the first position of the *chars_to_convert* string is matched to the first character in the *output_chars* string, the second character in the *chars_to_convert* string is matched to the second character in the *output_chars* string, and so on. If the *chars_to_convert* string is longer than the *output_chars* string, some characters will have no translation values.

Converting and Manipulating Boolean Values

XSLT and XPath define several functions that you can use to work with Boolean values. The main function you'll use is boolean(), which evaluates an expression and returns the result as a Boolean value, which is always either `true` or `false`. Consider the following example:

```
<xsl:value-of select="boolean($x > 5)"/>
```

If the variable x is greater than 5, the output from the boolean() function is `true`. Otherwise, if x is less than or equal to 5, the result is `false`.

Note XSLT processors convert the Boolean value (true or false) to a string for output. You don't need to explicitly call the string() function.

XSLT and XPath also include three utility functions that you can use to output Boolean values. These functions are

- **true()** Always returns the Boolean value `true`. You can use this during testing and development to test code branches and logic.
- **false()** Always returns the Boolean value `false`. You can use this during testing and development to test code branches and logic.
- **not()** Returns the negation of the expression. If the expression result isn't a Boolean value, it's converted to a boolean() value and then negated.

As stated, the true() and false() functions are best used during testing when you want to ensure that a branch of code is processed. For example, if you wanted to test the second when test in the following template:

```
<xsl:template match="item">
  <xsl:choose>
    <xsl:when test="stock/[@order='Y']">
      <p>Please order, stock number:
      <xsl:value-of select="@tracking_number"/>
     </p>
    </xsl:when>
    <xsl:when test="stock/[@order='N']">
      <p>Item <xsl:value-of select="@tracking_number"/>
      doesn't need to be re-stocked at this time.</p>
    </xsl:when>
    <xsl:otherwise>
      <p>INVALID ORDER INDICATOR FOR ITEM:
      <xsl:value-of select="@tracking_number"/>
      </p>
    </xsl:otherwise >
```

```
  </xsl:choose>
</xsl:template>
```

you could replace the first when test with false() and the second when test with true(), like this:

```
<xsl:template match="item">
  <xsl:choose>
    <xsl:when test="false()">
      <p>Please order, stock number:
      <xsl:value-of select="@tracking_number"/>
     </p>
    </xsl:when>
    <xsl:when test="true()">
      <p>Item <xsl:value-of select="@tracking_number"/>
      doesn't need to be re-stocked at this time.</p>
    </xsl:when>
    <xsl:otherwise>
      <p>INVALID ORDER INDICATOR FOR ITEM:
      <xsl:value-of select="@tracking_number"/>
      </p>
    </xsl:otherwise >
  </xsl:choose>
</xsl:template>
```

Because the first when test evaluates to `false`, the contents of this test aren't processed. The contents of the second when test, however, are processed. Here, the test evaluates to `true`, which tells the processor to process the contents of this when test.

The not() function is useful when you want to convert the results of an expression to a boolean value and then negate the results. In the following example, the value output is `false`:

```
<xsl:value-of select="not(true())"/>
```

Here, you tell the processor to return the opposite of `true`, which means the output is the value `false`.

The not() function is useful when want to evaluate complex logical expressions, such as those that use a logical And or a logical Or. Table 5-3 provides an overview of how you can use logical And, logical Or, and the not() function.

Table 5-3. Using Logical Expressions

Operation	Operator
logical AND	and Example: (true and false) `Result: false`
logical OR	or Example: (true or false) Result: true
Not	not() Example: not(false) Result: true

Logical And tests whether the first and the second expression are true. Both expressions must be true for the logical And to evaluate to true. Logical Or, on the other hand, tests whether one of two expressions is true. Only one expression must be true for the logical Or to evaluate to true. If you wanted to return the opposite result of a Logical And or a Logical Or, you could use the not() function to do this, such as:

```
<xsl:value-of select="not($x and $y)"/>
```

Using the true() Function

The true() function always returns the Boolean value `true`. You can use the true() function in your stylesheet by doing the following:

- As part of a select attribute or within another function, type **true()**.

Using the false() Function

The false() function always returns the Boolean value `false`. You can use the false() function in your stylesheet by doing the following:

- As part of a select attribute or within another function, type **false()**.

Using the not() Function

The not() function returns the negation of the expression passed as an argument. You can use the not() function in your stylesheet by doing the following:

- As part of a select attribute or within another function, type **not()**.

Working with Numeric Values

As with strings, XSLT and XPath define many functions you can use to work with numeric values. You can use these functions to

- Convert values to numbers
- Define formatting for numbers
- Round numbers
- Count the number of occurrences of something
- Total values

Converting Values to Numbers

You use the number() function to convert selected values to numbers. You can also use the number() function to convert parameter and variable values to numbers.

Table 5-4 provides a summary of the numeric conversion rules for various types of values. Boolean values, integers, floats, strings, and node sets are all converted in different ways.

Table 5-4. Value Conversion to Numbers

VALUE TYPE	CONVERSION DESCRIPTION
Boolean	Boolean values `true` and `false` are converted to the numbers 1 and 0, respectively. Example: 1
Node set	The first node in a node set is converted to a string as if it were passed to the string() function and then the result is converted to a number as with any other string. Details: Converts only the contents of the first node in node set
String	If the string contains only numeric values or a valid floating-point number that follows IEEE 754, the string is converted a floating-point value that's the nearest mathematical representation of the string. Otherwise, NaN is returned. Example: 7.5425

Most of the time, the XSLT processor will perform number conversions for you behind the scenes. For example, you specify that you want to output the product of $x and $y, which represent the variables x and y without having to explicitly convert the values, such as:

```
<xsl:value-of select="$x * $y"/>
```

If x is "5" and y is "12", the result is 60, which is output as a string. You can also explicitly convert values to numbers, such as:

```
<xsl:value-of select="number(false())"/>
```

Here, the output is 0, which is the numeric representation of false.

To convert a value to a number, do the following:

- As part of a select attribute or within another function, type **number(*expression*)**, where *expression* is an XPath expression that returns a node set or an actual value to convert.

Formatting Values as Numbers

XSLT and XPath define two structures that you can use to format values as numbers. These structures are

- **xsl:decimal-format** Can be used to set the default format for numbers and to define named alternative number formats
- **format-number()** Can be used to specify the exact formatting of a number and then represent it as string in the output

Techniques to work with these structures are discussed in the sections that follow.

Specifying the Number Formatting

You use the `xsl:decimal-format` element to define the default format for numbers as well as named formats that can be referenced from the format-number() function. This element is a top-level empty element that must always be used at the same level as your other top-level declarations in the stylesheet. The element has no required attributes.

Table 5-5 provides a summary of the optional attributes for the `xsl:decimal-format` element. If you don't set a format name for the element using the name attribute, the element is assumed to define the default number format for all output.

Table 5-5. Decimal Formatting Attributes

ATTRIBUTE	DESCRIPTION
name	Sets the name of the format, which can be referenced from the format-number() function. Example: name="format-1"
decimal-separator	Specifies the character used as the decimal point. With U.S. English, the decimal separator is a period (.), which is the default value. This character is used both in the format string and in the output. Example: decimal-separator=","

grouping-separator	Defines the character used as the thousands separator. With U.S. English, the grouping separator is a comma (,), which is the default value. This character is used both in the format string and in the output. Example: grouping-separator="."
infinity	Defines the string used to represent infinity. The string is only used in the output and has the default value "Infinity". Example: infinity="[out of bounds]"
minus-sign	Defines the character used as the minus sign. This character is only used in the output and has a hyphen (-) as the default value. Example: minus-sign="-"
NaN	Defines the string used to represent NaN. The string is only used in the output and has the default value "NaN". Example: NaN="[not a number]"
percent	Defines the character used as the percent sign. This character is only used in the output and has a hyphen (-) as the default value. Example: percent="%"
per-mile	Defines the character used as the per-mile (‰) sign. This character is used both in the format string and in the output. The default value is the Unicode per-mile character (#x2030). Example: per-mile="‰"
digit	Defines the character used in the format string to represent a digit. The default value is the number sign character (#). Example: digit="#"
pattern-separator	Defines the character used in the format string to separate the positive and negative subpatterns. The default value is the semicolon character (;). Example: pattern-separator=";"

The following example defines a default number format and two alternative number formats:

```
<xsl:stylesheet version="2.0"
  xmlns:xsl="http://www.w3.org/1999/XSL/Transform">

  <xsl:output method="html"/>

<xsl:decimal-format decimal-separator="." grouping-
separator=","
     infinity="[out of bounds]" minus-sign="-"
     NaN="[not a number]" percent="%" per-mile="‰"
     digit="#" pattern-separator=";" />

<xsl:decimal-format name="US" decimal-separator="."
     grouping-separator=","/>


<xsl:decimal-format name="UK" decimal-separator=","
     grouping-separator="."/>

...
</xsl:stylesheet>
```

The default number format specifies values for all possible attributes that can be used with format and output strings. The US format specifies that the decimal separator is a period (.) and the grouping separator is a comma (,), meaning numbers look like this: 5,000,250 or 52.254. The U.K. format specifies that the decimal separator is a comma (,) and the grouping separator is a period (.), meaning numbers look like this: 5.000.250 or 52,254.

To define a default or alternative number format for a stylesheet, follow these steps:

1. At the top-level of the stylesheet, type **<xsl:decimal-format**.
2. If you want to specify a name for the number format, type **name="*format_name*"**, where *format_name* is the name you'll use to reference the number format.
3. Add any additional attributes that you want to define.
4. Complete the element declaration by typing **/>**.

Defining Precise Output Format

Whenever you want to format a number in a precise manner, you can use the format-number() function to handle the task. This function accepts an input value, which can be an XPath expression whose value can be converted to a number and which then formats the number using the format pattern string you define. The function also has an optional third argument that you can use to specify the name of a previously defined decimal format. If a named format isn't specified, the default decimal format is used.

The basic syntax of the format-number() function is:

```
format-number(number, format_pattern_string,
named_decimal_format?)
```

where *number* is the number to be formatted (or an XPath expression whose value can be converted to a number), *format_pattern_string* is the actual format pattern string you want the processor to work with, and *named_decimal_format* is the optional designator for the named decimal format that you want to use to format the output.

Here's an example:

```
<xsl:value-of select="format-number(.,'$###,###.00')"/>
```

This example says to format the contents of the current node using the pattern string '$###,###.00'. If the node contains the value "2568.5", the output is the string "$2,568.50".

Table 5-6 summarizes the characters you can use as part of the format pattern string. Keep in mind that you can customize the actual characters used for the decimal separator, grouping separator, and pattern separator. You change these characters by defining a different value in the decimal format that's applicable.

Note For a detailed example using the format-number() function, see the section of this chapter entitled "Summing Values."

Table 5-6. Characters for Format Pattern Strings

PATTERN STRING CHARACTER	DESCRIPTION
#	Represents a digit where trailing and leading zeroes aren't displayed. Example: Formatting the value 51.0 with the pattern "####.##" returns the string "51".
0	Represents a digit where a zero is always displayed if provided in the input string. Example: Formatting the value 51.0 with the pattern "####.00" returns the string "51.00".
.	Represents the decimal point. Formatting a number with too few digits to the left and right of the decimal point doesn't result in automatic truncation. Example: Formatting the value 51.05 with the pattern "####.0" returns the string "51.05".
-	Represents the minus sign. Typically, used as part of the negative number pattern. Example: The following pattern string sets a positive and negative number pattern: "$###,###.##;-$###,###.##".
,	Represents the grouping separator. Example:

	Formatting 5005 with the pattern "$#,###.##" returns the string "$5,005".
;	Separates the positive and negative number pattern. Example: The following pattern string sets a positive and negative number pattern: "0,000.00;-0,000.00".
%	Indicates that a number should be represented as a percentage. The value will be multiplied by 100 and then displayed as a percentage. Example: Formatting the value .51 with the pattern "###.##%" returns the string "51%".
\u230	Represents the per-mile (‰) sign. The value will be multiplied by 1000 and then displayed as a per-mile. Example: Formatting the value .51 with the pattern "###.##\u230" returns the string "510‰".

To format numbers, follow these steps:

1. As part of a select attribute or within another function, type **format(*expression*,** where *expression* contains the number to be formatted.
2. Type **,'** (a comma followed by a single quotation mark).
3. Type the positive number pattern:

- Enter **$** if you want the value to represent dollars.
- Enter **0** for each digit that should always appear.
- Enter **#** for each digit that should only appear when it isn't zero.
- Enter **,** as the group separator character (or any other group separator character).
- Enter **.** as the decimal separator character (or any other decimal separator character).
- Enter **%** to multiply the number times 100 and display the result as a percentage.
- Enter **\u230** to multiply the number times 1000 and display the result as a per-mile.

4. Optionally, if you want to specify the negative number pattern, type the number pattern separator ; and then type – to indicate negative values. Use the same characters as specified in Step 2 to define the negative number pattern.
5. Type ' (a single quotation mark) to complete the number pattern string.
6. Optionally, type the name of the previously defined number format to use. Be sure to enclose the name in single quotation marks.
7. Type) to close the function.

The result should look similar to the following:

```
<xsl:value-of select="format-number(expression,
'$###,###.00-$###,###.00' 'format_name')"/>
```

Rounding Numbers

XSLT and XPath provide three functions for rounding numbers. These functions are

- **round()** Rounds to the nearest integer. A value of .5 in the decimal position always results in the number being rounded up. For example, round(1.5) results in 2 being written to the output.
- **ceiling()** Rounds up to the nearest integer. Any decimal value greater than .0 is rounded up to the next nearest integer. For example, ceiling(5.02) results in 5 being written to the output.
- **floor()** Rounds down to the nearest integer. Any decimal value is rounded down to the next nearest integer. For example, floor(1.92) results in 1 being written to the output.

The usage of round(), ceiling(), and floor() is the same. You pass the function a value, which can be an XPath expression. If the value isn't a number, the value is converted to a number as if it had been processed by the number() function. If the result of the conversion can be represented as a number, the value is rounded as appropriate for the function. If the result of the conversion is NaN, the output of the function is NaN.

In the following example, you round the contents of the current context node:

```
<xsl:value-of select="round(.)"/>
```

Using the round() Function

The round() function rounds to the nearest integer. You can use the round() function in your stylesheet by doing the following:

- As part of a select attribute or within another function, type **round(*number*)**, where *number* is the value that you want to round.

> **Note** A value of .5 in the decimal position always results in the number being rounded up. For example, round(100.5) results in 101 being written to the output.

Using the ceiling() Function

The ceiling() function rounds up to the nearest integer. You can use the ceiling() function in your stylesheet by doing the following:

- As part of a select attribute or within another function, type **ceiling(*number*)**, where *number* is the value that you want to round up to the next nearest integer.

> **Note** Any decimal value greater than .0 is rounded up to the next nearest integer. For example, ceiling(9.15) results in 10 being written to the output.

Using the floor() Function

The floor() function rounds down to the nearest integer. You can use the floor() function in your stylesheet by doing the following:

- As part of a select attribute or within another function, type **floor(*number*)**, where *number* is the value that you want to round down to the next nearest integer.

Note Any decimal value is rounded down to the next nearest integer. For example, floor(8.2) results in 8 being written to the output.

Summing Values

The most powerful yet simple function XSLT and XPath define has to be the sum() function. You use the sum() function to compute the total of all the numbers in a set of nodes. The single input argument for the function is the XPath expression that specifies the node set you want to total. If any node in the node set isn't a number, the value of the node is converted to a number as if it had been processed by the number() function. If the result of the conversion can be represented as a number, the value is added to the current total and the process continues. If the result of the conversion is NaN, the current total is set to NaN and the function returns this value.

The basic format of the sum() function is:

```
sum(expression)
```

where *expression* is an XPath expression that specifies the node set whose values you want to total. Following this, you could total the value of all the nodes in the current context like this:

```
<xsl:value-of select="sum(.)"/>
```

To get a better understanding of how you can use the sum() function with other functions, consider the following input document:

```
<?xml version="1.0"?>
<report>
  <title>Annual Royalty Summary for 2016</title>
  <quarter sequence="01">
    <books-sold>8503</books-sold>
    <royalty-earned>5210</royalty-earned>
  </quarter>
```

```
  <quarter sequence="02">
    <books-sold>5008</books-sold>
    <royalty-earned>2543</royalty-earned>
  </quarter>
  <quarter sequence="03">
    <books-sold>12759</books-sold>
    <royalty-earned>8540.5</royalty-earned>
  </quarter>
  <quarter sequence="04">
    <books-sold>9567</books-sold>
    <royalty-earned>6410.25</royalty-earned>
  </quarter>
</report>
```

The document represents an annual royalty summary for a particular book. As you can see, book sales and royalty earned are totaled on a quarterly basis. If you wanted to process the input document to create a formatted output document, you might want to reformat the text to achieve output similar to the following:

```
Quarter 1 - 8,503 books sold, $5,210.00 royalty earned.
```

The way you could do this is to examine the current sequence number and replace this value with the appropriate text designator, such as "Quarter 1". To do this, you'd have to define a set of elements in the XSLT stylesheet that contained the replacement values, such as:

```
<period sequence="01">Quarter 1</period>
<period sequence="02">Quarter 2</period>
<period sequence="03">Quarter 3</period>
<period sequence="04">Quarter 4</period>
```

Then you could insert these values as appropriate in the output document using a value-of select expression like this:

```
<xsl:value-of

select="document('')/*/period[@sequence=current()/@sequence]"/
>
```

Here, you specify that you want to select the sequence attribute of period elements in the current document as specified by document(“), which refers to the XSLT stylesheet itself, and replace @sequence=current() (meaning the current value of the sequence attribute in the current context node) with the contents of the element that has the matching sequence. If the current context node is the quarter element and the sequence value of the current node is "01", the replacement value is "Quarter 1".

Tip `document('')/*/period[@sequence=current()/@sequence]` may be a very complex expression, but it's still a basic predicate expression that follows the form *path[predicate]*, where *path* is the location path to the node that contains the desired subset of nodes you want to work with and *predicate* is the predicate expression that defines your filter for this set of nodes.

After you obtain the quarter designator, you can reformat the number of books sold and royalty earned values using the number-format() function. If you want to reformat the royalty earned for the current node in the node set, you could specify:

```
<xsl:value-of select="format-number(royalty-earned,
'$###,###.00')"/>
```

If you wanted to total all the royalty amounts and reformat the result, you could specify:

```
<xsl:value-of select="format-number(sum(//royalty-
earned),'$###,###.00')"/>
```

When you put all this together in a stylesheet, you'll end up with an .xsl file that looks like this:

```
<?xml version="1.0" ?>
<xsl:stylesheet version="2.0"
  xmlns:xsl="http://www.w3.org/1999/XSL/Transform">

  <xsl:output method="text"/>
```

```
  <xsl:variable name="newline">
<xsl:text>
</xsl:text>
  </xsl:variable>

  <period sequence="01">Quarter 1</period>
  <period sequence="02">Quarter 2</period>
  <period sequence="03">Quarter 3</period>
  <period sequence="04">Quarter 4</period>

  <xsl:template match="/">

    <xsl:value-of select="/report/title"/>
      <xsl:text>================================</xsl:text>
    <xsl:value-of select="$newline"/>
    <xsl:value-of select="$newline"/>

    <xsl:for-each select="report/quarter">
      <xsl:text>   </xsl:text>
      <xsl:value-of

select="document('')/*/period[@sequence=current()/@sequence]"/
>
      <xsl:text> - </xsl:text>
      <xsl:value-of select="format-number(books-sold,
'###,###')"/>
      <xsl:text> books sold, </xsl:text>
      <xsl:value-of select="format-number(royalty-earned,
'$###,###.00')"/>
      <xsl:text> royalty earned.</xsl:text>
      <xsl:value-of select="$newline"/>
      <xsl:value-of select="$newline"/>
    </xsl:for-each>
    <xsl:text>   Annual Totals: </xsl:text>
      <xsl:value-of select="$newline"/>
      <xsl:value-of select="$newline"/>
    <xsl:value-of select="format-number(sum(//books-sold),
'###,###')"/>
```

```
    <xsl:text> books sold, </xsl:text>
    <xsl:value-of
      select="format-number(sum(//royalty-
earned),'$###,###.00')"/>
    <xsl:text> royalty earned. </xsl:text>
  </xsl:template>

</xsl:stylesheet>
```

Based on this stylesheet and the previously specified input document, the output would look like this:

```
Annual Royalty Summary for 2016
===============================

   Quarter 1 - 8,503 books sold, $5,210.00 royalty earned.
   Quarter 2 - 5,008 books sold, $2,543.00 royalty earned.
   Quarter 3 - 12,759 books sold, $8,540.50 royalty earned.
   Quarter 4 - 9,567 books sold, $6,410.25 royalty earned.

   Annual Totals: 35,837 books sold, $22,703.75 royalty
earned.
```

You can use the sum() function in your stylesheet by following these steps:

1. As part of a select attribute or within another function, type **sum(*expression*)**, where *expression* is an XPath expression that specifies the node set whose values you want to total.
2. The result is the total of the values in the specified nodes.

> **Note** If any node in the node set isn't a number, the value of the node is converted to a number as if it had been processed by the number() function. If the result can't be represented as a number, the total is set to NaN and the function returns this value.

Chapter 6. Restructuring and Manipulating Documents

This chapter takes a detailed look at techniques you can use to work with document structures. As you'll learn, XSL Transformations (XSLT) and XML Path (XPath) define many elements and functions that you can use to manipulate document sets and subsets. You can, for example, define multiple input documents that should be merged into a single output document. You can also copy selected parts of documents and write the selections to the output.

Combining and Merging Documents

Of all the functions that XSLT and XPath define, the one function that really stands out is the document() function. The document() function is the one universal utility—the "Holy Grail"—that you'll find in all of XSLT. Simply put, you use the document() function to specify an external resource that you want to process in the stylesheet, and this allows you to use a stylesheet to merge multiple documents and manipulate the contents of those documents just as you do the contents of a single document.

Document Merging Essentials

The document() function has the basic form:

```
document(resource)
```

where *resource* specifies the Uniform Resource Identifier (URI) path to the resource file you want to work with. You can also specify the node set within the resource file using the form:

```
document(resource/node-set)
```

such as:

```
document(order1115-0001.xml/purchase_order)
```

The second form is the more typical usage.

To see how you can merge documents, consider the following example:

```
<?xml version="1.0" ?>
<purchase_order>
   <customer>
      <account_id>10-487</account_id>
      <name>
         <first> William </first>
         <mi> R </mi>
         <last> Stanek </last>
      </name>
   </customer>
   <inventory>
     <item tracking_number="459320" manufacturer="MHSA">
        <item_type>Fiberglass Prehung Entry Door</item_type>
        <description>6-panel left-hand inswing entry door,
primed, white</description>
        <purchase quantity="50" unit_price="159.95" />
     </item>
     <item tracking_number="459378" manufacturer="TMH">
        <item_type>Steel Prehung Entry Door</item_type>
        <description>4-panel left-hand inswing entry door,
primed, black, steel</description>
        <purchase quantity="20" unit_price="179.95" />
     </item>
   </inventory>
</purchase_order>
```

Here, you've defined a purchase order in terms of a customer and the inventory items the customer is purchasing. If you had dozens or hundreds of such documents that you wanted to process, you could create a master document that referenced all the purchase orders that you wanted to work with and then use the document() function to process them.

The master document might look like this:

```
<master_doc>
  <title>Daily Purchase: November 15, 2016</title>
  <order filename="order1115-0001.xml"/>
```

```
  <order filename="order1115-0002.xml"/>
  <order filename="order1115-0003.xml"/>
  <order filename="order1115-0004.xml"/>
  <order filename="order1115-0005.xml"/>
  <order filename="order1115-0006.xml"/>
  <order filename="order1115-0007.xml"/>
  <order filename="order1115-0008.xml"/>
  <order filename="order1115-0009.xml"/>
  <order filename="order1115-0010.xml"/>
</master_doc>
```

You could then create a template rule within your stylesheet that examines the contents of each file in turn. Basically, you'd define an `xsl:for-each` element that selected the `master_doc/order` element in the master document and then called the document() function. The basic outline for this stylesheet would look like this:

```
<?xml version="1.0"?>
<xsl:stylesheet version="2.0"
  xmlns:xsl="http://www.w3.org/1999/XSL/Transform">

  <xsl:template match="/">
    <xsl:for-each select="/master_doc/order">
      <xsl:apply-templates
select="document(@filename)/purchase_order"/>
    </xsl:for-each>
  </xsl:template>

  <xsl:template match="purchase_order">
  ...
  </xsl:template>

</xsl:stylesheet>
```

Here, the document() function extracts the filename attribute for the order element and uses this value to set the URI path. Afterward, the function call specifies that the node set you want to work with is `/purchase_order`. The result is that the apply-templates selection is interpreted as:

- order1115-0001.xml/purchase_order on the first pass
- order1115-0002.xml/purchase_order on the second pass
- order1115-0003.xml/purchase_order on the third pass
- ...
- order1115-0010.xml/purchase_order on the tenth and final pass

As a result, the purchase_order template rule is called with the content node set defined as the contents of each document in turn. The really good news is that once you have a node set, you can work with it just as you do other node sets.

A key thing to note with the document() function is that you don't need to extract the entire contents of files. You can just as easily specify that you want to work with a subset of the document. To do this, simply specify the URI/node-set path that represents the node set that you want to work with. For example, with the previous documents, you could have processed only `customer` and `inventory` elements separately. Here's an example:

```
<?xml version="1.0" ?>
<xsl:stylesheet version="2.0"
  xmlns:xsl="http://www.w3.org/1999/XSL/Transform">

  <xsl:template match="/">
    <xsl:for-each select="/master_doc/order">
      <xsl:apply-templates
      select="document(@filename)/purchase_order/customer"/>
    </xsl:for-each>

    <xsl:for-each select="/master_doc/order">
      <xsl:apply-templates
      select="document(@filename)/purchase_order/inventory"/>
    </xsl:for-each>

  </xsl:template>

  <xsl:template match="purchase_order">
  ...
  </xsl:template>
```

```
</xsl:stylesheet>
```

Using Base Paths with the document() Function

The document() function has an additional form that you can use if you want to specify a base URI path to work with and then specify relative paths for the remaining resources. Here, you use the document() function with two arguments:

```
document(baseURI, resource)
```

where *baseURI* is the base URI path that you want to use and *resource* references the relative path to the resource that you want to work with. The relative path can include an XPath expression that specifies the node set within the resource as well.

To see how this additional form of the document() function works, let's continue the previous example where we want to merge multiple documents and then work with their contents. The master document could have been defined to specify the absolute path to the documents you wanted to work with, such as:

```
<master_doc>
  <title>Daily Purchase: November 15, 2016</title>
  <order filename="http://www.microsoft.com/data/order1115-
0001.xml"/>
  <order filename="http://www.microsoft.com/data/order1115-
0002.xml"/>
  <order filename="http://www.microsoft.com/data/order1115-
0003.xml"/>
  <order filename="http://www.microsoft.com/data/order1115-
0004.xml"/>
  <order filename="http://www.microsoft.com/data/order1115-
0005.xml"/>
  <order filename="http://www.microsoft.com/data/order1115-
0006.xml"/>
  <order filename="http://www.microsoft.com/data/order1115-
0007.xml"/>
  <order filename="http://www.microsoft.com/data/order1115-
0008.xml"/>
  <order filename="http://www.microsoft.com/data/order1115-
0009.xml"/>
```

```
  <order filename="http://www.microsoft.com/data/order1115-
0010.xml"/>
</master_doc>
```

More commonly, however, you might want to specify a base location for the documents and then use relative URLs, such as:

```
<master_doc>
  <title>Daily Purchase: November 15, 2016</title>
  <base_loc location="http://www.microsoft.com/data/" />
  <order filename="order1115-0001.xml"/>
  <order filename="order1115-0002.xml"/>
  <order filename="order1115-0003.xml"/>
  <order filename="order1115-0004.xml"/>
  <order filename="order1115-0005.xml"/>
  <order filename="order1115-0006.xml"/>
  <order filename="order1115-0007.xml"/>
  <order filename="order1115-0008.xml"/>
  <order filename="order1115-0009.xml"/>
  <order filename="order1115-0010.xml"/>
</master_doc>
```

If there's a base location referenced in the master document, you could reference this value when calling the document() function. Here's an example:

```
<?xml version="1.0"?>
<xsl:stylesheet version="2.0"
  xmlns:xsl="http://www.w3.org/1999/XSL/Transform">

  <xsl:template match="/">

    <xsl:for-each select="/master_doc/order">
      <xsl:apply-templates
select="document(/master_doc/base_loc/@location,
@filename)/purchase_order"/>
    </xsl:for-each>
  </xsl:template>
```

```
  <xsl:template match="purchase_order">
  ...
  </xsl:template>

</xsl:stylesheet>
```

In this example you obtain the base URI by obtaining the value of the location attribute in the master document's base_loc element.

Using the document() Function

You can use the document() function to process elements declared in the XSLT stylesheet using the form:

```
document('')
```

In the section of Chapter 5 ("Working with Strings, Booleans, & Numbers") entitled "Summing Values," you saw an example of this reference. There, an input document was defined like this:

```
<?xml version="1.0"?>
<report>
  <title>Annual Royalty Summary for 2016</title>
  <quarter sequence="01">
    <books-sold>8503</books-sold>
    <royalty-earned>5210</royalty-earned>
  </quarter>
  <quarter sequence="02">
    <books-sold>5008</books-sold>
    <royalty-earned>2543</royalty-earned>
  </quarter>
  <quarter sequence="03">
    <books-sold>12759</books-sold>
    <royalty-earned>8540.5</royalty-earned>
  </quarter>
  <quarter sequence="04">
    <books-sold>9567</books-sold>
    <royalty-earned>6410.25</royalty-earned>
```

```
  </quarter>
</report>
```

and you needed to define elements in the stylesheet to act as translation values for the sequence attributes that the input document declared. These elements were defined as:

```
<period sequence="01">Quarter 1</period>
<period sequence="02">Quarter 2</period>
<period sequence="03">Quarter 3</period>
<period sequence="04">Quarter 4</period>
```

You then used an empty path reference for the document() function to allow the elements to be processed. The reference looked like this:

```
<xsl:value-of

select="document('')/*/period[@sequence=current()/@sequence]"/
>
```

If you used this declaration in a minimal stylesheet like this:

```
<?xml version="1.0" ?>
<xsl:stylesheet version="2.0"
  xmlns:xsl="http://www.w3.org/1999/XSL/Transform">

  <xsl:output method="text"/>

  <period sequence="01">Quarter 1</period>
  <period sequence="02">Quarter 2</period>
  <period sequence="03">Quarter 3</period>
  <period sequence="04">Quarter 4</period>

  <xsl:template match="/">
    <xsl:for-each select="report/quarter">
      <xsl:value-of

select="document('')/*/period[@sequence=current()/@sequence]"/
>
      <xsl:text>
```

```
</xsl:text>
    </xsl:for-each>
  </xsl:template>

</xsl:stylesheet>
```

the output of processing the input document is:

```
Quarter 1
Quarter 2
Quarter 3
Quarter 4
```

Here, the sequence values in the input document are replaced with the contents of the `period` elements defined in the stylesheet.

Declaring the document() Function

Now that you know a bit about the document() function, you're probably ready to use it in your own stylesheets. To do that, follow these steps:

1. As part of a select attribute or within another function, type **document(*resource*)** or **document(*baseURI resource*)**, where *baseURI* is the base URI path that you want to use and *resource* references the relative path to the resource that you want to work with. The relative path can include an XPath expression that specifies the node set within the resource as well.
2. The function returns the node set within the specified document that you referenced.

Manipulating Document Structures

XSLT and XPath define many additional constructs that you can use to manipulate document structures. The key constructs are

- xsl:copy
- xsl:copy-of
- xsl:element

- xsl:attribute
- xsl:attribute-set

Techniques you can use to work with these elements are discussed in the following sections.

Creating Copies of Node Sets

The `xsl:copy` element copies the current node and its namespace nodes to the output tree. It doesn't copy attribute nodes or any text nodes of the current node. You can think of this as a shallow copy. To see how this works, consider the following XSLT stylesheet that makes a copy of all the elements in the input document:

```
<xsl:stylesheet version="2.0"
  xmlns:xsl="http://www.w3.org/1999/XSL/Transform">

  <xsl:output method="xml"/>

  <xsl:template match="*">
   <xsl:copy>
     <xsl:apply-templates/>
   </xsl:copy>
  </xsl:template>

</xsl:stylesheet>
```

If this is the input document:

```
<?xml version="1.0" ?>
<inventory>
   <item tracking_number="459320" manufacturer="MHWB
Industries">
      <item_type>Fiberglass Prehung Entry Door</item_type>
      <description>6-panel left-hand inswing entry door,
primed, white</description>
      <stock in_stock="750" orders_for="200" net_units="550"
order="N" />
   </item>
   <item tracking_number="459323" manufacturer="Not listed">
```

```
      <item_type>Fiberglass Prehung Entry Door</item_type>
      <description>6-panel left-hand inswing entry door,
primed, white</description>
      <stock in_stock="50" orders_for="200" net_units="-150"
order="Y" />
   </item>
   <item tracking_number="459780" manufacturer="MHWB
Industries">
      <item_type>Steel Prehung Entry Door</item_type>
      <description>4-panel left-hand inswing entry door,
primed, black, steel</description>
      <stock in_stock="250" orders_for="200" net_units="50"
order="Y" />
   </item>
   <item tracking_number="459789" manufacturer="Not listed">
      <item_type>Steel Prehung Entry Door</item_type>
      <description>4-panel left-hand inswing entry door,
primed, black, steel</description>
      <stock in_stock="0" orders_for="200" net_units="-200"
order="Y" />
   </item>
</inventory>
```

the resulting output document looks like this:

```
<?xml version="1.0" encoding="UTF-8"?>
<inventory>
   <item>
      <item_type>Fiberglass Prehung Entry Door</item_type>
      <description>6-panel left-hand inswing entry door,
primed, white</description>
      <stock />
   </item>
   <item>
      <item_type>Fiberglass Prehung Entry Door</item_type>
      <description>6-panel left-hand inswing entry door,
primed, white</description>
      <stock />
   </item>
```

```
   <item>
      <item_type>Steel Prehung Entry Door</item_type>
      <description>4-panel left-hand inswing entry door,
primed, black, steel</description>
      <stock />
   </item>
   <item>
      <item_type>Steel Prehung Entry Door</item_type>
      <description>4-panel left-hand inswing entry door,
primed, black, steel</description>
      <stock />
   </item>
</inventory>
```

Essentially, the document is stripped of all nodes except for element and namespace nodes. The `xsl:copy` element has an optional attribute called use-attribute-sets that allows you to define a list of one or more attribute sets that the `xsl:copy` element should use to add attributes to the selected output elements. If you used this attribute with the previously defined stylesheet, you'd have to copy elements individually and then apply the appropriate attribute set to the element. However, it would probably be easier to just use the `xsl:copy-of` element to perform this task. The `xsl:copy-of` element copies a selected node and all its associated nodes to the output tree.

The select attribute is the only attribute that you can use with `xsl:copy-of` element. select is a required attribute that defines the XPath expression that you want to match. This means that if you defined the following template for the same input document:

```
<xsl:stylesheet version="2.0"
  xmlns:xsl="http://www.w3.org/1999/XSL/Transform">

  <xsl:output method="xml"/>

  <xsl:template match="/">
   <new_root>
    <xsl:copy-of select="item">
   </new_root>
  </xsl:template>
```

```
</xsl:stylesheet>
```

the resulting output would look like this:

```
<?xml version="1.0" encoding="UTF-8"?>
<new_root>
   <item tracking_number="459320" manufacturer="MHWB
Industries">
      <item_type>Fiberglass Prehung Entry Door</item_type>
      <description>6-panel left-hand inswing entry door,
primed, white</description>
      <stock in_stock="750" orders_for="200" net_units="550"
order="N" />
   </item>
   <item tracking_number="459323" manufacturer="Not listed">
      <item_type>Fiberglass Prehung Entry Door</item_type>
      <description>6-panel left-hand inswing entry door,
primed, white</description>
      <stock in_stock="50" orders_for="200" net_units="-150"
order="Y" />
   </item>
   <item tracking_number="459780" manufacturer="MHWB
Industries">
      <item_type>Steel Prehung Entry Door</item_type>
      <description>4-panel left-hand inswing entry door,
primed, black, steel</description>
      <stock in_stock="250" orders_for="200" net_units="50"
order="Y" />
   </item>
   <item tracking_number="459789" manufacturer="Not listed">
      <item_type>Steel Prehung Entry Door</item_type>
      <description>4-panel left-hand inswing entry door,
primed, black, steel</description>
      <stock in_stock="0" orders_for="200" net_units="-200"
order="Y" />
   </item>
</new_root>
```

To perform a shallow copy of a node set, follow these steps:

1. Type <xsl:copy>.
2. Type **<xsl:apply-templates select="*expression*" />**, where expression identifies the node that you want to copy.
3. Type </xsl:copy>.
4. The contents of the specified node and any child element nodes it contains are copied to the output tree. Although copies are also made of namespace nodes, attribute, text, comment, and processing-instruction nodes aren't copied.

To perform a deep copy of a node set, follow these steps:

1. Type **<xsl:copy-of select="*expression*" />**, where expression identifies the node that you want to copy in its entirety.
2. The contents of the specified node and all child nodes it contains are copied to the output tree.

Generating Elements and Attributes

Anytime you want to generate elements or attributes in an output document, you'll use `xsl:element`, `xsl:attribute`, and `xsl:attribute-set` to handle the task.

Using xsl:element

`xsl:element` has three attributes:

- **name** A required attribute that sets the name of the element you want to generate.
- **namespace** An optional attribute that sets the namespace for the element.
- **use-attribute-sets** An optional attribute that defines a list of one or more attribute sets that should be used with elements of this type. Each attribute set name must be separated with a space.

You'll often use `xsl:element` to define a new name for an existing element or to extract data from multiple sources and put it into a single element. To see how this works, consider the following example:

```
<item_type>Fiberglass Prehung Entry Door</item_type>
<description>6-panel left-hand inswing entry door, primed,
white</description>
```

```
<stock in_stock="50" orders_for="200" net_units="-150"
order="Y" />
```

Here we have three separate elements definitions. If you wanted to create a single element that contained all this data, you could specify:

```
<xsl:template match="item|description|stock">
  <xsl:element name="data">
    <xsl:value-of select".|@*"/>
    <xsl:text>;</xsl:text>
  </xsl:element>
</xsl:template>
```

The output is now formatted as an element with a list of values separated by semicolons:

```
<data>Fiberglass Prehung Entry Door;6-panel left-hand inswing
entry door, primed, white;
50;200;-150;Y</data>
```

One of the most common uses of `xsl:element` is to convert all attributes in an input document to elements in an output document. A stylesheet that handles this task looks like this:

```
<?xml version="1.0"?>
<xsl:stylesheet version="2.0"
  xmlns:xsl="http://www.w3.org/1999/XSL/Transform">

  <xsl:output method="xml"/>

  <xsl:template match="*">
    <xsl:element name="{name()}">
      <xsl:for-each select="@*">
        <xsl:element name="{name()}">
          <xsl:value-of select="."/>
        </xsl:element>
      </xsl:for-each>
      <xsl:apply-templates select="*|text()"/>
    </xsl:element>
```

```
  </xsl:template>

</xsl:stylesheet>
```

This stylesheet processes every element in the input document. Each element in the input document is examined in turn. If the element has attributes, an element with the same name as the attribute is created with its value set to the attribute's current value. After processing the element's attributes, the stylesheet processes any child or text nodes that the element contains. Following this, if the input document looked like this:

```
<?xml version="1.0" ?>
<inventory>
   <item tracking_number="459320" manufacturer="MHWB
Industries">
      <item_type>Fiberglass Prehung Entry Door</item_type>
      <description>6-panel left-hand inswing entry door,
primed, white</description>
      <stock in_stock="750" orders_for="200" net_units="550"
order="N" />
   </item>
</inventory>
```

the output using the stylesheet would look similar to this:

```
<?xml version="1.0" encoding="UTF-8"?>
<inventory>
   <item>
      <tracking_number>459320</tracking_number>
      <manufacturer>MHWB Industries</manufacturer>
      <item_type>Fiberglass Prehung Entry Door</item_type>
      <description>6-panel left-hand inswing entry door,
primed, white</description>
      <stock>
        <in_stock>750</in_stock>
        <orders_for>200</orders_for>
        <net_units>550</net_units>
        <order>N</order>
       </stock>
```

```
  </item>
</inventory>
```

To generate an element in the output, complete the following steps:

1. In the template rule that you want to use to output the element, type **<xsl:element name="*element_name*"**, where *element_name* is the actual name of the element you want to create.
2. Optionally, type **namespace="*namespace*"**, where *namespace* references the element's namespace prefix.
3. Optionally, type **use-attribute-sets="*attribsSet*"**, where *attribsSet* is a space-separated list of one or more attribute sets that should be used with elements of this type.
4. As necessary, enter any declarations that set the element's contents.
5. Type </xsl:element>.

The result should look similar to the following:

```
<xsl:element name="element_name">
...
</xsl:element>
```

Using xsl:attribute-set and xsl:attribute

You use `xsl:attribute-set` to define a set of attributes that you want to add to elements that you're generating. The basic form of an attribute set is:

```
<xsl:attribute-set name="attribute_set_name">
  <xsl:attribute name="attribute1_name">value1</xsl:attribute>
  <xsl:attribute name="attribute2_name">value2</xsl:attribute>
...
  <xsl:attribute name="attributeN_name">valueN</xsl:attribute>
</xsl:attribute-set>
```

where *attribute_set_name* is the name of the attribute set; *attribute1_name, attribute2_name, ...*, and *attributeN_name* are the names of the attributes you want to define; and *value1, value2, ..., valueN* are the values for those attributes.

The basic form can be extended:

- If you want to associate another attribute set with the current attribute set, you can set the optional use-attribute-sets attribute. The value for this attribute is the name of the attribute set to use.
- If you need to define a namespace for the attributes, you can set the optional namespace attribute of the `xsl:attribute` element. The value of this attribute is the name you want to use.

Generating attributes is useful when you're defining new elements with fixed attribute values. For example, if you had the following input:

```
<stock>
  <stock_year>2016</stock_year>
  <company>Microsoft</company>
  <stock_for>2016</stock_for>
</stock>
```

and wanted to create output structured like this:

```
<stock stock="2016" company="Microsoft" stock_for="2016" />
```

you could define an attribute set like this:

```
<xsl:attribute-set name="stockAttribs">
  <xsl:attribute name="stock_year">2016</xsl:attribute>
  <xsl:attribute name="company">Microsoft</xsl:attribute>
  <xsl:attribute name="stock_for">2016</xsl:attribute>
</xsl:attribute-set>
```

You could then generate an element that contained these fixed value attributes, like this:

```
<xsl:element name="stock" use-attribute-set="stockAttribs"/>
```

Of course, this technique only works when there are fixed values that you want to use. If the values aren't fixed, however, you'll want to generate the attributes as the elements are being processed. For example, if the typical stock element looked like this:

```
<stock>
  <in_stock>750</in_stock>
  <orders_for>200</orders_for>
  <net_units>550</net_units>
  <order>N</order>
</stock>
```

and you wanted to create output structured like this:

```
<stock stock="750" orders_for="200" net_units="550" order="N"
/>
```

you could define a template rule to transform the original element set like this:

```
<xsl:template match="stock">
  <xsl:element name="stock">
    <xsl:for-each select="*">
      <xsl:attribute name="{name()}">
        <xsl:value-of select="."/>
      </xsl:attribute>
    </xsl:for-each>
  </xsl:element>
</xsl:template>
```

This template creates a new element called `stock` and processes every child element of the original `stock` element, transforming them into attributes. Each child element is created as a like-named attribute with its value set to the current value of the child element.

To define an attribute set, complete the following steps:

1. At the top-level of the stylesheet, type **<xsl:attribute-set name="*attribute_set_name*">**, where *attribute_set_name* is the actual name of the attribute set.
2. Type **<xsl:attribute name="*attribute_name*">**, where *attribute_name* sets the name of the attribute you're defining.
3. As necessary, enter any declarations that set the attribute's contents.
4. Type </xsl:attribute>.
5. Repeat steps 2-4 to define other attributes for this attribute set.

6. Type **</xsl:attribute-set>** to complete the attribute set definition.

To generate individual attributes as part of an element you're defining, follow these steps:

1. In the template rule that you want to use to output the element, type **<xsl:element name="*element_name*"**, where *element_name* is the actual name of the element you want to create.
2. Optionally, type **namespace="*namespace*"**, where *namespace* references the element's namespace prefix.
3. As necessary, enter any declarations that set the element's contents.
4. Type **<xsl:attribute name="*attribute_name*">**, where *attribute_name* sets the name of the attribute you're defining.
5. As necessary, enter any declarations that set the attribute's contents.
6. Type </xsl:attribute>.
7. Repeat steps 4-6 to define other attributes for this attribute set.
8. As necessary, enter any declarations that complete the element's contents.
9. Type </xsl:element>.

The result should look similar to the following:

```
<xsl:element name="element_name">
  ...
    <xsl:attribute name="{name()}">
      ...
    </xsl:attribute>
  ...
</xsl:element>
```

Sorting Document Structures

So far this chapter has looked at ways you can manipulate document structures and perform various tasks. Up until now, you've always worked with structures in the order in which they were defined in the original input document and used this selection order to determine what the output looked like. Earlier in the book, however, I promised you that you could use XSLT and XPath to perform many advanced tasks, including sorting alphabetically and numerically. Now it's time to discuss how sorting works.

Sorting Essentials

The XSLT structure you use to sort nodes is xsl:sort. The xsl:sort element has several attributes that you can use. These attribute are

- **select** An XPath expression that defines the node set you want to sort. The selection can include any type of node, not just element nodes. This means you could sort by attribute values or by the values of other node types.
- **data-type** Sets the sort type. Valid values include data-type="text" for alphabetic sorts and data-type="number" for numeric sorts.
- **order** Sets the sort order as either ascending or descending. The default order is order="ascending".
- **case-order** Sets the letter case sort order. By default, the letter case isn't used to determine the order of the sort. This means an uppercase A and a lowercase a have the same sort value. However, if you want the processor to differentiate between uppercase and lowercase letters, you can specify the letter case sort order as case-order="upper-first" or case-order="lower-first". With case-order="upper-first", uppercase letters sort first. With case-order="lower-first", lower case letters sort first.
- **lang** Sets the language of the sort keys. For example, if the language is U.S. English, you could specify lang="us".

None of these attributes are required and the default sort order is a forward alphabetic sort.

The basic format of the sort element is:

```
<xsl:sort select="expression"/>
```

where *expression* is an XPath expression that specifies the node set you want to sort.

You can define the `xsl:sort` element inside `xsl:for-each` and `xsl:apply-templates` elements. Within `xsl:for-each` elements, the `xsl:sort` must appear immediately after the opening tag <xsl:for-each>. Otherwise a processor exception occurs.

Defining Sort Keys, Order, and Type

You use the `xsl:sort` element to reorganize selected nodes alphabetically or numerically. Each `xsl:sort` that you define acts as a sort key, meaning you can have a primary sort key, a secondary sort key, a tertiary sort key, and so on. To see how powerful this can be, consider the following example:

```
<?xml version="1.0" standalone="no"?>
<!DOCTYPE purchase_order PUBLIC "-//Stanek//PO
Specification//EN"
         "http://www.tvpress.com/pospec.dtd">
<accounts>
   <customer>
      <account_id>10487</account_id>
      <name>
         <first>William</first>
         <mi>R</mi>
         <last>Stanek</last>
      </name>
   </customer>
   <customer>
      <account_id>09685</account_id>
      <name>
         <first>Robert</first>
         <mi>W</mi>
         <last>Stanek</last>
      </name>
   </customer>
   <customer>
      <account_id>11285</account_id>
      <name>
         <first>William</first>
         <mi>A</mi>
         <last>Stanek</last>
      </name>
   </customer>
</accounts>
```

Here we have a list of accounts that contain the keyword "Stanek," which was returned as an XML document from the corporate database. Although there are only three customer entries in this example, you can imagine a case where there are hundreds or thousands of customer entries—perhaps the account representative entered "William" as the keyword or wanted a list of all accounts.

To make this information useful, the data needs to be sorted in a specific order. One way to sort the data would be by `account_id`. Since this is a numerical value, you'd want to sort the `account_id` as a number. Here's an example stylesheet that sorts the `accounts` by `account_id`:

```
<?xml version="1.0"?>
<xsl:stylesheet version="1.0"
     xmlns:xsl="http://www.w3.org/1999/XSL/Transform">

  <xsl:output method="text" indent="no"/>
  <xsl:strip-space elements="*"/>

  <xsl:variable name="newline">
<xsl:text>
</xsl:text>
  </xsl:variable>

  <xsl:template match="/">
    <xsl:for-each select="accounts/customer">
      <xsl:sort select="account_id" data-type="number"/>
      <xsl:value-of select="account_id"/>
      <xsl:text> : </xsl:text>
      <xsl:value-of select="name/first"/>
      <xsl:text> </xsl:text>
      <xsl:value-of select="name/mi"/>
      <xsl:text>. </xsl:text>
      <xsl:value-of select="name/last"/>
      <xsl:value-of select="$newline"/>
    </xsl:for-each>
  </xsl:template>
</xsl:stylesheet>
```

The sort is accomplished using the `xsl:sort` element with a selection by `account_id`. This means that `account_id` is the primary sort key. The data-type for the sort is set to number, which tells the XSLT processor to sort the values as numbers. The resulting output looks like this:

```
09685 : Robert W. Stanek
10487 : William R. Stanek
11285 : William A. Stanek
```

In this example the `xsl:sort` element is defined inside an `xsl:for-each` element. `xsl:sort` can also appear inside `xsl:apply-templates` elements. Within `xsl:for-each` elements, the `xsl:sort` must appear immediately after the opening tag <xsl:for-each>. Otherwise a processor exception occurs.

The default sort order is ascending, which you could explicitly set using:

```
<xsl:sort select="account_id" data-type="number"
order="ascending"/>
```

You could also specify descending order, such as:

```
<xsl:sort select="account_id" data-type="number"
order="descending"/>
```

Now the account numbers are listed from highest to lowest, such as:

```
11285 : William A. Stanek
10487 : William R. Stanek
09685 : Robert W. Stanek
```

Another way to sort a list of accounts would be to sort by last name and then by first name. This would mean the sort would have two keys: name/last and name/first. Using the same input document, you could rewrite the stylesheet to use two sort keys like this:

```
<?xml version="1.0"?>
<xsl:stylesheet version="2.0"
  xmlns:xsl="http://www.w3.org/1999/XSL/Transform">
```

```
  <xsl:output method="text" indent="no"/>
  <xsl:strip-space elements="*"/>

  <xsl:variable name="newline">
<xsl:text>
</xsl:text>
  </xsl:variable>

  <xsl:template match="/">
    <xsl:for-each select="accounts/customer">
      <xsl:sort select="name/last"/>
      <xsl:sort select="name/first"/>
      <xsl:value-of select="name/last"/>
      <xsl:text>, </xsl:text>
      <xsl:value-of select="name/first"/>
      <xsl:text> </xsl:text>
      <xsl:value-of select="name/mi"/>
      <xsl:text>. </xsl:text>
      <xsl:value-of select="account_id"/>
      <xsl:value-of select="$newline"/>
    </xsl:for-each>
  </xsl:template>
</xsl:stylesheet>
```

Using the new stylesheet, the output looks like this:

```
Stanek, Robert W. 09685
Stanek, William R. 10487
Stanek, William A. 11285
```

If you were paying particular attention to this sort, you noticed that it isn't quite perfect yet. That's because William R. Stanek appears before William A. Stanek in the output. The reason for this is that that was the original order in the input document and you didn't sort the customer list by middle initial. You can resolve this problem by adding a third sort key. The new stylesheet looks like this:

```
<?xml version="1.0"?>
<xsl:stylesheet version="2.0"
```

```
  xmlns:xsl="http://www.w3.org/1999/XSL/Transform">

  <xsl:output method="text" indent="no"/>
  <xsl:strip-space elements="*"/>

  <xsl:variable name="newline">
<xsl:text>
</xsl:text>
  </xsl:variable>

  <xsl:template match="/">
    <xsl:for-each select="accounts/customer">
      <xsl:sort select="name/last"/>
      <xsl:sort select="name/first"/>
      <xsl:sort select="name/mi"/>
      <xsl:value-of select="name/last"/>
      <xsl:text>, </xsl:text>
      <xsl:value-of select="name/first"/>
      <xsl:text> </xsl:text>
      <xsl:value-of select="name/mi"/>
      <xsl:text>. </xsl:text>
      <xsl:value-of select="account_id"/>
      <xsl:value-of select="$newline"/>
    </xsl:for-each>
  </xsl:template>
</xsl:stylesheet>
```

And the output is exactly what is expected:

```
Stanek, Robert W. 09685
Stanek, William A. 11285
Stanek, William R. 10487
```

Forward alphabetic sorts are the default sort type, but you can also specify an alphabetical sort explicitly. Here's an example:

```
<xsl:sort select="account_id" data-type="text"
order="ascending"/>
```

As with numeric sorts, you can do reverse alphabetic sorts. Here's an example:

```
<xsl:sort select="account_id" data-type="text"
order="descending"/>
```

Sorting Nodes in a Document

Now that you know how to work with `xsl:sort`, you can specify the nodes to sort in a document by following these steps:

1. You can define the `xsl:sort` element inside `xsl:for-each` and `xsl:apply-templates` elements. Within `xsl:for-each` elements, the `xsl:sort` must appear immediately after the opening tag <xsl:for-each>. Otherwise a processor exception occurs.
2. Type **<xsl:sort select="*expression*"**, where *expression* is an XPath expression that specifies the node set you want to sort.
3. Optionally, type **order="descending"** to set descending order for the sort. order="ascending" is the default value.
4. Optionally, type **data-type="number"** to specify a numeric sort. The default is data-type="text" for a text sort.
5. Optionally, with a text sort, type **case-order="upper-first"** to sort uppercase letters first or type **case-order="lower-first"** to sort lowercase letters first.
6. Type **/>** to complete the xsl:sort element.
7. Repeat steps 2-6 to define additional sort keys.

Note The first sort key created is the primary sort key. The second key is the secondary sort key and so on.

Counting Nodes

Any time you need to count the number of nodes in a node set, you can use the count() function to do this. For example, let's say you had an XML document that contained all the purchase orders for the day in the form:

```
<?xml version="1.0"?>
```

```
<purchase_order>
  <order>...</order>
  <order>...</order>
  <order>...</order>
  <order>...</order>
</purchase_order>
```

and you wanted to output the total number of orders in the document. You could do this by defining a value-of declaration in the root node that counted the number of order nodes, such as:

```
<xsl:template match="/">
  <text>The total number of orders is: </text>
    <xsl:value-of select="count(order)"/>
  <text>.</text>
</xsl:template>
```

The output is then:

```
The total number of orders is: 4.
```

If the summary document had three different types of orders, you might want to total orders in a different way. Here, you could total individual order types and also determine the total number orders of any type. To see how this works, consider the following example XML document:

```
<?xml version="1.0"?>
<purchase_order>
  <order type="walkin">...</order>
  <order type="phone">...</order>
  <order type="web">...</order>
  <order type="walkin">...</order>
</purchase_order>
```

Here you have three order types: walkin, phone, and web. With this in mind, you could define a template to count these order types and to provide a total of all orders, like this:

```
  <xsl:variable name="newline">
```

```
<xsl:text>
</xsl:text>
  </xsl:variable>

<xsl:template match="/">
  <text>
Daily Order Summary
===================
</text>

  <text>  Total Walk-in Orders: </text>
  <xsl:value-of select="count(order/@type='walkin')"/>
  <xsl:value-of select="$newline"/>

  <text>  Total Phone Orders: </text>
  <xsl:value-of select="count(order/@type='phone')"/>
  <xsl:value-of select="$newline"/>

  <text>  Total Online Orders: </text>
  <xsl:value-of select="count(order/@type='web')"/>
  <xsl:value-of select="$newline"/>
  <xsl:value-of select="$newline"/>

  <text>
Daily Order Total
=================

  Total orders: </text>
    <xsl:value-of select="count(order)"/>
  <text>
=================</text>



</xsl:template>
```

and the output would look like this:

```
Daily Order Summary
===================

  Total Walk-in Orders: 2
  Total Phone Orders: 1
  Total Online Orders: 1

Daily Order Total
=================

  Total orders: 4
=================
```

To count nodes, complete the following steps:

1. As part of a select attribute or within another function, type **count(*expression*)**, where *expression* is an XPath expression that specifies the node set whose nodes you want to count.
2. The result is the number of nodes in the node set.

Thank you!

Thank you for purchasing *XSL: The Personal Trainer*! This text was designed to help you get started with XSL. Don't forget to review what you've learned and refer back to sections of the text as appropriate to help you with your further studies.

Contents in Review

About the Author

William R. Stanek (http://www.williamstanek.com/) has more than 20 years of hands-on experience with advanced programming and development. He is a leading technology expert, an award-winning author, and a pretty-darn-good instructional trainer. Over the years, his practical advice has helped millions of programmers, developers, and network engineers all over the world. His current and books include *Windows Administration Pocket Consultant*, *Windows Server 2012 R2 Pocket Consultant* and *Windows Server 2012 R2 Inside Out.*

William has been involved in the commercial Internet community since 1991. His core business and technology experience comes from more than 11 years of military service. He has substantial experience in developing server technology, encryption, and Internet solutions. He has written many technical white papers and training courses on a wide variety of topics. He frequently serves as a subject matter expert and consultant.

William has an MS with distinction in information systems and a BS in computer science, magna cum laude. He is proud to have served in the Persian Gulf War as a combat crewmember on an electronic warfare aircraft. He flew on numerous combat missions into Iraq and was awarded nine medals for his wartime service, including one of the United States of America's highest flying honors, the Air Force Distinguished Flying Cross. Currently, he resides in the Pacific Northwest with his wife and children.

William recently rediscovered his love of the great outdoors. When he's not writing, he can be found hiking, biking, backpacking, traveling, or trekking in search of adventure with his family!

Find William on Twitter at www.twitter.com/WilliamStanek and on Facebook at www.facebook.com/William.Stanek.Author.

THE BOOK YOU NEED TO GET UP TO SPEED™

THE PERSONAL TRAINER™

XML, DTDs, SCHEMAS

WILLIAM STANEK

Award-winning technology expert

www.ingramcontent.com/pod-product-compliance
Lightning Source LLC
Chambersburg PA
CBHW080410060326
40689CB00019B/4200
* 9 7 8 1 5 1 8 8 4 5 3 5 2 *